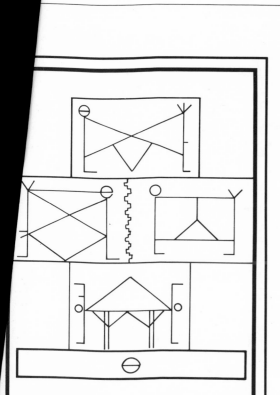

PLATE I   Level

Arts on the Level

The Fall
of the Elite Object

BY MURRAY KRIEGER

UNIVERSITY OF TENNESSEE PRESS
KNOXVILLE

Other Books by Murray Krieger

Poetic Presence and Illusion: Essays in Critical History
and Theory
Directions for Criticism: Structuralism and Its
Alternatives (co-editor with L. S. Dembo)
Theory of Criticism: A Tradition and Its System
The Classic Vision: The Retreat from Extremity in
Modern Literature
The Play and Place of Criticism
Northrop Frye in Modern Criticism (editor)
A Window to Criticism: Shakespeare's *Sonnets* and
Modern Poetics
The Tragic Vision: Variations on a Theme in Literary
Interpretation
The New Apologists for Poetry
The Problems of Aesthetics (co-editor with Eliseo Vivas)

Library of Congress Cataloging in Publication Data

Krieger, Murray, 1923–
Arts on the level.

(The Hodges lectures)
1. Aesthetics—Addresses, essays, lectures.
2. Criticism—Addresses, essays, lectures. I. Title.
II. Series: Hodges lectures.
BH39.K68   700'.1   80-25401
ISBN 0-87049-308-6

CONTENTS

EMBLEMS (by Joan Krieger)

v

PREFACE

The chapters that follow were prepared as the John C. Hodges Lectures and were delivered on successive nights at the University of Tennessee in early October 1979. I have resisted the temptation to expand the lectures, even where expansion seemed called for, out of a desire to be faithful to the original occasion to which they were addressed. For the same reason I have preserved the lecture format and the rhetorical flavor consistent with oral delivery.

My immediate justification for these decisions is quite personal: thanks to my hosts, I found the occasion of my visit to the university and my delivery of these lectures so pleasant that I relished this prospect of preserving it in the essentially unaltered testimony of these pages. But I believe there also is a justification more related to the essential character of the lectures: in conceiving of the series as a structural unit, it functioned for me—much as a novella does for the writer of fiction—as an extended work beyond the scope of an essay and yet more compact in its argument than the full-blown theoretical treatise I normally seek to produce. I found this unit an attractive size that could serve me well, so I wanted to preserve its trim lines by resisting the urge to extend them.

As a consequence of my decision not to enlarge upon my lectures, the reader will find that my statements of positions and historical tendencies in aesthetics and criticism of the arts are usually generalized, so that they do not often enough name and deal with individual writers and works as representative of those positions and tendencies. In order to resist the stretching out of my remarks by the detailed analyses of writers and writings, I may sometimes allow statements to stand without the differentiations that the study of particulars would introduce. Such is the price of what I feel is gained by the limits I decided to maintain. One further constraint operated to reinforce these limits: since these lectures were intended for a general university audience, I tried to compose them with that audience in mind, to make them more broadly accessible than my other work, which has been addressed to specialists in criticism and theory. Thus, I wanted to avoid bogging down my arguments in small technical issues and too much specification about individual names and works. I choose to assume that the audience I had (and have) in mind would prefer that I not inhibit the brisk pace I try to set for my argument.

But general readers should be aware of at least one departure from their usual expectations: as I use the word "poem," it has a special meaning. As a technical shorthand common to works in literary theory, the term "poem" is synonymous with Aristotelian *poesis,* giving the term a broadened meaning to cover all "imaginative" literature, or fictions, whether written in verse or prose. Undoubtedly there are other lapses into recent theoretical jargon, but this was the one habitual offense that I felt required a special note here.

In composing these lectures, I tried to give my arguments a historical grounding, in contrast to my usual sources of argument, which tend to be exclusively theoretical. Yet my own theoretical bias has doubtless intruded upon my historical recital. And in the end that bias is all-controlling, perhaps seeking to undo the course of history and where it has brought us. Indeed, this theoretical attempt to overcome history underlies my objective in writing these lectures. For I confess my faith in theory as a creation that constitutes our response to the human need to impose form on our historical experience: theory may not be able to change history or the future, but it can keep us from being nothing but history's victims.

These lectures were mainly written in 1978 while I served as a Rockefeller Foundation Humanities Fellow. I should like to thank the Rockefeller Foundation for permitting me the freedom and the travel out of which the following pages emerged.

In expressing my desire to reproduce here the original occasion of these lectures, I should mention the one exception I have made, the one addition to my original contribution. To an occasion addressed to auditors I am delighted now to add a visual supplement, the emblems created by my wife, Joan Krieger—one for the entire book (on the frontispiece) and one for each of the three chapters. Since she shared the ideas in the lectures with me, it is gratifying to see those ideas seized in the emblems for graphic display. The division in the spirit of the lectures I find reflected in the split, in her emblems for each of the chapters, between the constructive and the deconstructive impulses in history. I thank her for helping me develop the ideas in this book and, with her emblems, for making the book complete.

Finally, I should like to revert to what I said at the start about the pleasurable nature of the occasion sponsored by the Department of English and the Administration of the University of Tennessee. Those who heard me were attentive and receptive, but they also were so vigorously responsive that I was persuaded to make some adjustments in my remarks (usually in the form of supplementary footnotes) to take account of their probing comments. For the warmth of their hospitality and the keenness of their participation I am deeply grateful.

—MURRAY KRIEGER
February 1980
Laguna Beach, California

Arts on the Level

PLATE 2   Museum ⟩ (Muse)um

1. THE PRECIOUS OBJECT:
FETISH AS AESTHETIC

There is nothing more pleasing to a traveller—or more terrible to
travel-writers, than a large rich plain; especially if it is without rivers or
bridges; and presents nothing to the eye, but one unvaried picture of
plenty: for after they have once told you that 'tis delicious! or delightful!
(as the case happens)—that the soil was grateful, and that nature pours
out all her abundance, etc. . . . . they have then a large plain upon their
hands, which they know not what to do with—and which is of little or no
use to them but to carry them to some town; and that town, perhaps of
little more, but a new place to start from to the next plain—and so on.
—This is most terrible work; judge if I don't manage my plains better.

TRISTRAM SHANDY, Vol. VII, Chap. 42

I begin with a discourse, perhaps in the end more serious than it
may seem along the way, about the word "level." That word is
central to the title of these lectures and to their subject: what are the
consequences to the arts—and to criticism of the arts—of contemporary efforts to level them, to make all artistic productions level
with one another, to reduce them all to a dead level? Please note that
in the question I have just asked I have used the one word as verb, as
adjective, and as noun indifferently, since its meaning remains the
same whatever its usage. Even the idiomatic phrase I have borrowed
for my title ("on the level")—with its meaning of unexceptional,
unvarying, you-know-where-to-have-it reliability—requires no
slightest shift in our sense of the word, so that the idiom has an
immediately transparent meaning consistent with the unchanging
character of "level." What I am trying to say, I suppose, is that the
word's usage is as flatly uniform as its meaning.

But there is something yet more extraordinary in this word's insistence on its dead-sameness. Let me ask you to be visually playful with
the word as a sequence of printed letters. I suggest that "level" is a
unique example in our language of a word that is a graphic emblem of
its meaning. (I have avoided beginning this sentence with the word
since capitalizing the "l"—as I was forced to do in my title—destroys

3

the symmetry of its graphic image. I hope also—as a result of my special pleading with editor and printer—to have the word appear, when I talk about it as a word, between quotation marks instead of in the more usual italics, because I want the word to appear without having it lean in any one direction, in order to preserve the purity of its noncommittal character.) So I set forth the word "level," uncapitalized and in roman, as a word that—as it is printed in this text—presents itself as having a literal appearance that signifies what it conventionally means. The most obvious fact about the word's appearance is that it is identical read forward or backward. But the case is more unusual than this: the word is bounded, left and right, by simple uprights (the two lower-case "l"'s, and the less serif on the "l" the better); interior to each upright is the character-less vowel, and at the center sits the "v" on its inverted fulcrum, sending forth its two legs equally in either direction. (A fanatic pursuit of my animated figure suggests that the letter "v" itself can sit securely on its midpoint only on ground that is itself level.)

What makes the appearance of "level" so striking is the utter, dead-even indiscriminateness, which is the word's conventional meaning. I am saying, in effect, that in this one instance the word is a natural as well as an arbitrary sign, and that its two ways of meaning are—metaphorically at least—identical. And of course this is not how verbal signs function, although—through whatever historical accidents of its etymology—it is how this one does. Given the meaning of "level," so reinforced—or even duplicated!—by its graphic appearance, the case is rather amazing. The word, like its meaning, is always the same, without the promise of change or surprise; indeed, it is its own guarantee of literal monotony. To be "level" is nothing less than to be at all times parallel to the horizon. The lack of variation, the equality in height of all entities on the plane, must be absolute when things are truly, justly, honestly, on the level (and here the idiom and the literal prepositional phrase come to the same thing). It may be even more maddening to learn—as we have a moment ago—that we can move from verb to adjective to noun without changing our sense of the word's constancy of meaning. Thus "level" is just the word and the graphic form to embody, as it signifies, its unvaryingly uniform state—and the state in any of the entities that it may be used to describe. Is it any wonder that I write these essays in terror over the

4

consequences to the arts of having them placed "on the level" these days? For I can think of no human activity so dedicated to the exceptional and to the elevated as the arts are. But this is to get ahead of the argument.

I did not mean to tarry as long as I have in this pictographic analysis, which may well border on Addisonian "false wit," with its intense examination of letters and words as visual images. Nor would I have dwelled so long upon it except for my own dread of "level" as a topographical characteristic. I remember spending too much of my life in a level part of the midwest, a broad tableland that made a nearby town named "Rising" the butt of a local joke in which we accused it of wishful thinking. We used to wonder what human dynamics could occur in an area where, left unattended and undisturbed, a ball might not move an inch from year to year. It is not surprising that, since I fled that place, I have at all costs sought homes on higher ground from which to view the more level (though still variegated, *not* level) land below.

So the word "level" is of no importance, nor is the way I have been toying with it, except that its remarkable, and yet irritating, reflexive nature—its endless self-reinforcement—may urge our increasing awareness of the deadly dangers of arts on the level. I have used the word to provide an emblematic notion of the total unelevated character, and the monotonous consequences, of the anti-elitist view of the arts and humanistic studies. This view, which is gaining a larger following these days, tries to impose itself on how we are to create art as well as how we are to judge that which was created in less anti-elitist days. I shall be primarily concerned with this desire in our culture to include the arts in our impulse to be egalitarian in all things. In light of the dread, dead state of being "level," what ought our consternation to be as we witness the leveling operation of the leveler operating in the realm of the arts? We must—as I shall try to do before my third lecture is complete—press him to the logical consequences of his leveling intention, to force him to be—and to leave him—on the level.

There is a long-standing precedent in the history of literature and criticism for my metaphorical concern with levels and rises.[1] One

---

[1]And in the history of politics too, I should add, pointing to the Levelers in seventeenth-century Parliamentary England, who may well have set the precedent for the frequently political character of the anti-elitist leveling in the arts being traced in these lectures.

could write a lengthy treatise on mountain imagery and plain or flatland imagery, and on the human values and concerns attaching to each. From the muses' Helicon in ancient Greece to Thomas Mann's *Magic Mountain*, mountains have been associated with the unpredictable dynamics of human creativity. It is the "flatland" mentality that, as in Mann, threatens to drag all creativity down to its dead level. We can think, for example, of Alexander Pope's *Essay on Criticism* where, at the outset of Part Two, he represents the critic, inspired by "what the muse imparts," climbing one set of Alps after another as he seeks to scale "the heights of Arts." This passage is in tone with Pope's earlier praise for the poet as Pegasus, who chooses to "deviate from the common track" (that is, the track on level ground, on the level). It is this passage on the young critic's journey through the Alps that Dr. Johnson calls "perhaps the best [simile] that English poetry can show."

Wordsworth, acting out the role set forth in Pope's simile, is appropriately captivated by mountains, sensing them as a source of energy to be emphatically shared by the traveler among them. He recalls for us the strength imparted to his imagination by his journey across the Alps (*The Prelude*, Book 6) and his climb up Mount Snowden (Book 14). It is not just a matter of high versus low: valleys and even abysses are also of great psychic value for him, since they are—as neighbors to hillier terrain—part of a "variegated journey":

And Earth did change her images and forms
Before us, fast as clouds are changed in heaven.
Day after day, up early and down late,
From hill to vale we dropped, from vale to hill
Mounted. . . .   (Book 6; 490–496)

The climax of such variety occurs for him in the Simplon Pass (lines 621–640), in which the extreme forms of nature's opposites lead the poet to an apocalyptic moment.

By way of contrast, Wordsworth experiences landscape on the level in his poem on "Salisbury Plain," that "desolate" flatland with nothing but "cornfields stretched and stretching without bound" (line 26). In his definitive study of Wordsworth, Geoffrey Hartman comments on the "horror of the horizontal" in these lines, the "distinct sense of horizontal infinity . . . extended in 'stretched and stretching' to become almost a grammatical figure." The "horizontal appears as

6

an expansion of the static."[2] The sense of endless, undemarcated space is easily transferred into the sense of endless, undemarcated time, a notion enhanced by Wordsworth's own reminder to us (in his prefatory Advertisement to the poem) of the "monuments and traces of antiquity" found in Salisbury Plain (Stonehenge, of course). This horizontal infinity (of time as well as space?) is what, in the poem, makes the place so empty a waste, an unbroken, unvaried, and endless ("stretched and stretching") plain that threatens to stifle the human imagination. We are back to Tristram Shandy's better-humored struggle with his plain (as he describes it in my epigraph), and we look forward to Thomas Mann's notion of the "flatland," the land-sea that is a dull infinity of time and space unelevated by imagination out of its universal sameness.

What may well be involved in these symbolic uses of mountain and plain is the romantic mind's antipathy (in the name of the single lofty genius and his imagination) to reducing all being to a single level. Pope, in a more neo-classical mood than that represented by the references I made earlier, sets forth such a flatland reduction in his lines, from his *Essay on Man*, in which his God, "with equal eye, as God of all," can see "A hero perish, or a sparrow fall, / Atoms or systems into ruin hurled, / And now a bubble burst, and now a world" (Epistle I, lines 87–90). The "equal eye" of his God is a level, and leveling, eye; it demonstrates precisely how the leveling act becomes the equalizing act. The parallel structures themselves effect the leveling; in uniting the important with the trivial, they lead to the rhetorical figure of *zeugma*, which yokes the two together by forcing them into the reduced grasp of the single verb ("hurled," "burst"). There is something paradoxical in so stratified and class-conscious a vision as that of the "great chain of being" finding a single principle of structure that dissolves the hierarchy on which it is based, reducing all the levels to one universally same existence on the level.

This neo-classical universality, using its "equal eye" to oversee an all-inclusive refusal to differentiate, deeply disturbs the romantic sensibility. The romantic need to soar beyond the common level of life often translates into bird as well as mountain imagery. The number of poems in which such a will to soar occurs is of course very great. That

[2]*Wordsworth's Poetry 1787–1814* (New Haven: Yale University Press, 1964), p. 119.

anti-romantic critic, T. E. Hulme, comments on this romantic penchant for heights in his "Romanticism and Classicism": "You might say if you wished that the whole of the romantic attitude seems to crystallise in verse round metaphors of flight. Hugo is always flying, flying over abysses, flying up into the eternal gases."[3] Finally, whether the metaphors are of flight or of mountain climbing, the romantic imagination is seeking a way to insist upon its specialness, its isolated freedom from flatland ordinariness. In the early twentieth century, the distinguished critic Clive Bell, a cool formalist hardly thought of as a romantic, joins this metaphorical tradition: gladly, he tells us, he disdains "the snug foothills of warm humanity" in order to join the few "who have climbed the cold, white peaks of art."[4]

We could multiply indefinitely examples from literature and criticism which, through metaphor, place art in a transcendent isolation, breathing its own rarefied atmosphere far above our pedestrian realities. But it is more important for my purposes to examine the historical moment at which theorizing in aesthetics projects such notions into a formal system, since I want, in the balance of this lecture, to set forth the elitist aesthetic in order to establish the theoretical structure against which the anti-elitist program of leveling has been directed. By the late eighteenth century the work of Immanuel Kant created as much of a Copernican revolution in aesthetics as he is often credited with creating in metaphysics and theory of knowledge. His aesthetic was to a great extent a systematizing of the impulse I have been tracing in metaphor—the impulse to isolate art on a lofty pinnacle and to approach it in a distinct way in order to discover the special powers that it has created for itself in its isolation.

Despite the static hierarchy in earlier eighteenth-century thought (that which preceded Kant's so-called critical philosophy), a hierarchy that was eminently supportive of class structure and elites, the earlier neo-classical doctrine did not call for the separation of art from other human interests. Quite the contrary. The strongly held doctrine of *ut pictura poesis* insisted on keeping the arts together as "sister arts" and saw them as similarly dedicated to the imitation of those universals

[3]*Speculations: Essays on Humanism and the Philosophy of Art,* ed. Herbert Read (London: Routledge & Kegan Paul, Ltd., 1924), p. 120.
[4]These are in the final lines of the opening chapter of Clive Bell's *Art* (London: Chatto & Windus, 1914).

that the period philosophy affirmed to hold all reality together. Differences in the media of the several arts were overridden by the unity of their mimetic objective. Further, art's role of picturing the universals that structure reality easily translated into a didactic function that was to accompany the descriptive function.

It is clear that, in such a concept, art is deeply and yet immediately tied to our workaday world, although it is equally clear that, in defining these functions, such theory is talking only about art's "content" and not its "form." The assimilation of all the arts to a single definition of purpose necessarily precludes our concern with how any one of them manipulates its medium in order to create the special sort of object the particular art is capable of creating. (We can note the title of the treatise by the Abbé Charles Batteux, *The Fine Arts Reduced to a Single Principle* [1746]. This admitted reduction is clearly an early attempt to put all the arts on the level, this time under the "equal eye" of imitation, through an ambitious extension of the doctrine of *ut pictura poesis*.) Further, the monolithic interest in the imitative capacity of all the arts leads us at once from what goes on inside the object to its "object of imitation" outside. Indeed, in using the clause "what goes on inside the object," I am being anachronistic, since we cannot really talk about the work itself as an "object" in the eighteenth century before Kant. The only objects we then have are those "objects of imitation" that furnish the prior reality that the art work is to transpose into itself without significant alteration. For such alteration would require a concentration on the manipulative role of the medium that would create an integral object with its own special reality—a concept reserved for aesthetics in the wake of Kant. Without special attention to the medium—and hence to distinctions instead of analogies among the arts—trans*pos*ition cannot become trans*form*ation; the objects remain outside to be imitated without an object of its own being constructed from inside. So the work remained a collection of imitated objects rather than being an integral object itself. It was a collection of contents, and one could view form only as a superficial imposition upon these contents, an afterthought. Consequently, in most eighteenth-century theory before Kant, the price of the nonisolation of the arts from life was that each art was deprived of any special way of functioning, of using its medium to put its form and content together into a unique presentational configuration.

Early in Kant's *Critique of Judgment* (1790), the keynote was sounded with the concept of disinterestedness. Giving systematic development to notions hinted at by Hutcheson and Mendelssohn, among earlier theorists, Kant was able to found an aesthetic that formulated aesthetic objects that could be kept at a distance from the mundane interests of their audience, so that such objects, intended for disinterested satisfaction, could seek their own autonomy. It was, of course, the way in which he fit the aesthetic into the entire structure of his thought that permitted Kant to find this separate role for art. Through his restriction of "pure reason" to the cognitive realm, narrowly conceived (what we can *know*), and his restriction of "practical reason" to the moral realm (the realm of action, the arena of "interest"), he left to the aesthetic the interest-free realm that allowed the art object to pursue its self-sufficiency.

Yet that self-sufficiency could find itself, in his formulation of the "beautiful," as subservient to the principle of form—that is, subservient to the construction of an object that fulfilled the demands of a total internal purposiveness. It is formal purposiveness that for Kant is the transcendental principle that our formal habit of mind must project as the basis for the organization of the universe, so that it must be purposiveness that we seek to find—and want our artists to place into their objects for us to find—if those objects are to satisfy our aesthetic needs, whose disinterestedness must seek a self-sufficient stimulus. So we have the apparently paradoxical—but really not at all paradoxical—notion of disinterested purposiveness, which means only an internal purposiveness that relates to no external interest, but only to its own internally generated formal demands, thus leading to an audience satisfaction free of the satisfaction of any desire. And in the object we have at work a satisfying teleology—not altogether unlike Aristotle's, if on utterly different grounds—that allows the object to come to terms with itself under a principle of closure, thereby sealing itself off from the world and its interests. Clearly the theoretical stage has been set for the development of the varieties of formalistic or near-formalistic aesthetics that increasingly sacralized (or, if one takes the demystifying attitude, that increasingly fetishized) the aesthetic object, until this development realized perhaps its fullest expression in the New Criticism.

But, besides the aesthetic of Kant, there were necessarily other major elements working to free the art object and to isolate it as an autonomous entity. One might say that many things happened in the life of the mind and of society at much the same time, some of them calling for a position like Kant's and others perhaps deriving from such positions. We must, for example, constantly remind ourselves that only with Alexander Gottlieb Baumgarten, in the middle of the eighteenth century, was "aesthetics," as a discipline, named and given its place.[5] The setting aside of this domain must seem, in retrospect, to call forth a doctrine that justifies such a political move within the traditional disciplines and their competitive imperialisms by setting aside the aesthetic experience and the aesthetic object. The late eighteenth century is also the moment of revolutions in thought and deed that propelled into being a different kind of audience for the arts.

We also trace to this period—largely as a result of this new audience—the emerging concept of the museum as a public art gallery, in which objects are segregated for isolated scrutiny as art. This development has enormous implications about the way in which art works function in their culture. Churches may still serve as repositories of an art that, however magnificent, is clearly subservient to religion and to theological realities, for the church is where such art belongs. Its doctrine is the root whose flower is the art, and to witness religious art in the church is to experience it in the full context that gives it its meaning. There can be no questioning the relationship between the art object and its living environment.

It is obvious enough that an increasingly secular art finds the museum to be its equivalent of a church, though one that must be shared with a miscellaneous aggregation of religious objects that have lost their homes and now find asylum in the museum. But it should be at least as obvious that the relationship between the museum and its contents is far more arbitrary than that between the church and its contents. The works in the museum, as general art gallery, must be self-justifying—asking to be perceived for their own sakes since there is no other reason for them to be there soliciting our attention. Nor is there any reason for us to visit the place at all except for the individual value of its contents. In days before the growth and multiplication of

---

[5]Baumgarten, *Aesthetics* (1750), and an earlier, youthful forecast of it in *Philosophical Thoughts on Matters Pertaining to Poetry* (1735).

museums (exclusively a nineteenth- and twentieth-century phenomenon), even secular art objects, except when seized by conquerors, usually were displayed in places associated with their production—by patrons and in great homes and palaces. There has been a similar drift of these objects to those great orphan asylums, the monumental public galleries of the world.[6]

In this movement to museums, what we have, in other words, is the deracination of art objects. Brought together (or bought together) from many times and nations and civilizations all over the world and human history, art objects have been cut off from their sources in the human life and culture that nourished their creation. The fact is that the greatest of our European collections have been gathered through the ruthless looting of imperialist conquest, and our American collections gathered through the acquisitive instincts of robber barons who would brook no competition in their purchases. And this fact only argues the more strongly for the arbitrary character of these collections of objects—objects that, increasingly with this movement of collecting, have only their own (supposedly) intrinsic value to justify their capture, or their purchase, and their display. And surely the continuously rising monetary value of these objects is more and more a manifestation of this intrinsic value and—with it—pride of purchase and ownership, even if only to serve the public. Totally out of relation to their home or to the occasion of their display, these art works have been cut off from performing any vital cultural function; instead, they are to keep their lonely spot in the hall and show themselves, with only an extraneous label to place them superficially in time and culture. These are indeed museums *with* walls, sealed off from societies to which their contents do not relate anyway. If they are shrines to the arts, the idols within must contain their sacred character within the nature of their own fabrication. For, as they hang, they relate to nothing and to no place or time.

The movement into museums, it can be argued, moves through the "art for art's sake" notions of the nineteenth century and finds its final theoretical expression in those American New Critics, who created an admirable machine for the exhaustive analysis of each isolated poem

[6]The public concert hall, which carried music out of its home in church and chamber, could be shown as having a development analogous to that of the public art gallery.

as the ultimate artifact—a kind of *art trouvé* that functioned fully, though apart from author or audience or culture. The anthology of such poems was to be our museum, now collected without pain from the poetic assemblage of the ages, though on the theoretical model that museums had presented for us in the plastic arts. And the stimulus in aesthetics for museum and anthology was, I repeat, the Kantian notion of disinterestedness, leading to the need to maintain "aesthetic distance" (distance between object and subject of aesthetic experience and distance between object and its sources in man and culture), and from there to autonomy and self-sufficiency of the object (through the internally exploited principle of a purposiveness free of any external interest).

The reification of those systems of signs that our interpretive energy converts into aesthetic objects is now complete, and we proceed to idolize them. We have set firm boundaries around the objects we have projected into being (as if we learned, and decided to justify, why we have set frames around paintings); by so doing we have made them into special objects, illuminated by their self-directed purposiveness from within. The objects are thus treated as self-enclosures, as totalizations, with a self-fulfillment that raises them above all non-aesthetic human fabrications (however strong the interest these fabrications satisfy). In this way objects of art have become elite objects for us, beyond the common level of objects that—responsive to interests beyond themselves—are not finally objects at all but, instead, flow beyond themselves into the interests they serve.

Art criticism deriving from this elitist aesthetic must take its method from its need to reveal what makes its special object so special, what turns an artifact into art, with all the exemptions and the privilege conferred by the term "art." Somehow the artist has worked the medium into paths which, in its recalcitrance, the medium would normally not take; and this deviation opens opportunities for exploitation that allow the object to achieve its unique closure. Criticism must seek to follow and account for this process, in whichever of the arts it is serving. Hence the critic, concentrating on the medium, is concerned with those tangible elements in the art object that give it its material being, that solid reality that the museum collects, thereby setting it aside for us to visit and admire.

Our culture has thus converted these objects into our fetishes, claiming them to be worthy of our secular worship; and museums, filled with them, do indeed become the churches of the secular world. If the objects within have been collected as autonomous individuals in order to be made into aesthetic idols, then obviously their material reality is indispensable; and the physical media of the plastic arts, as they are manipulated by artists who construct their precious objects out of them, would have to become central features of an aesthetic concerned with accounting for the formal purposiveness—and hence the internal self-sufficiency—of such objects. In other words, the emergence of aesthetic vision out of the artist's struggles with the medium is properly a central concern in any attempt to account for the unique character of the object that we have made elite by segregating it from its culture for worship in the museum.

To those of us in literature, much of my presentation may well appear troublesome. We wish literary objects to share the aesthetic characteristics of objects in the other arts, and, indeed, I seemed to be assuming as much when I suggested that the New Criticism represented a final stage in the tendency—which I attributed to the museum movement and to Kant—to rip art free of its cultural roots and to treat art objects as already (as we come upon them) fully formed members of an ideal miscellaneous anthology. But the emphasis I have been placing on the art object as a tangible entity capable of being materially valued, of being collected and displayed, would appear to put poems and fictions at a disadvantage, if not altogether out of consideration. The question of the medium of the language arts has always been fraught with difficulties, but never so much before the dominance of an aesthetic that gave so primary a role to the material medium. It is very likely for these reasons that the major literary aesthetic after Kant (say, from Coleridge to the New Criticism) spends much of its energy seeking to create a medium for poetry that will allow it to be treated analogously to the plastic arts in an aesthetic that pays tribute to the human power to demonstrate its mastery over a recalcitrant medium.

Please do not misunderstand: nothing that any literary aesthetician can do is going to turn the poem into a materially precious object. The word's spiritual—or at least immaterial, airy—appeal does not permit us to speak of it as a medium except metaphorically, does not permit us to see the poet working like the sculptor or painter except by rough analogy that must preserve a keen awareness of the differences between the poet and the others. I am only trying to say that the elevation of art objects into precious objects, as the result of the transformed attitudes toward art arising during the later eighteenth century, profoundly affected literary theory by forcing it also to find a way of making its object truly an "object"; as the result of an aesthetic devoted to autonomous objects of art, literary theory began, by contagion as it were, to search for a material (or a metaphorically material) basis for the poem, even though no one was seriously anticipating turning the poem into a collectable object. (As I have suggested, the post-New-Critical anthology of poems is as close to a museum as we are likely to come.)[7] The aesthetic, one might argue, spread out beyond the realm (of materially precious aesthetic objects) in whose special interest it seemed to be directing its motivating energy.

How, then, can literary theorists find the means for their subject to thrive in its competition with the other arts despite its lacking the requisite medium that has been central to the development of the aesthetics of the arts in the past two centuries? We can answer by looking first at the inadequacy of language as a medium and then by seeing what literary artists can do about that inadequacy in order to make language serve them as a medium after all. Language presents difficulties to the poet as artist both for what it does not have that plastic media have and for what it has that plastic media do not have. On the one side, as we have observed, words, as conventional signifiers, have no body, no material substance: they have meaning, but no being. This lack of body leads to the other side of their difference from clay or stone and from paint-and-canvas, which have being without meaning (at least no meaning until they are fashioned into art): words are already fully formed elements in common use, with agreed-upon meanings, before they are picked up for use by the poet. An aesthetic medium is usually regarded as a neutral element ready to be manipulated into meaning by the artist. But such is not the case with words, which, instead of presenting the material resistance of other media, come already fully laden with relatively stable mean-

---

[7]It should hardly be necessary for me to add that I am speaking only of poems and not of "books" as physical entities. The latter, at their material best, are as collectable as art objects in the museum. Clearly, what gives to books their value as collectables is related to them as objects of the plastic arts and is not related to their verbal content.

ings. (Now it is certainly true that the media of the plastic arts are not totally neutral: there are tendencies for certain colors or intensities of color, or certain shapes, to produce common responses in viewers. And the artist must accept and work within such given a priori limitations. Within some conventions there are also iconographic givens for the artist to accept before beginning work. Still, such restrictions are surely general and permissive when compared to the precise and arbitrary fixities of given verbal meanings and the worlds into which they open as we read our sentences, whether in the news-paper or in a poem.)

I repeat the other difficulty of words as medium: the price of their being assigned fixed, prior meanings is that words are deprived of any material reality, of body. The only thing we can do with a painting hanging on the wall of a museum is to look at it—to try to look at it as a painting, bringing all our aesthetic habits of perception to the task. So the only use the painting can be put to is determined by our response to what the artist has done in the creation of it. As I have written elsewhere, we do not attempt to eat the oranges off a still-life canvas, knowing them to be only illusions within a painterly tradition. But many readers of poems do try to make practical use of the words in their pre-poetic state, wrongly treating them as if they were the usual words and constituted declarative sentences in another sort of discourse—treating words, that is, as if they were *not* functioning as an aesthetic medium. This is why teachers of literature often have difficulty teaching uninitiated students—who insist they already know how to read—how to read poems. It is because these students presum-ably "know how to read" that they have so much to unlearn before they can read language as an aesthetic medium. Teachers of art ap-preciation should have many fewer complications in initiating their students—even fewer when they are dealing with non-rep-resentational paintings, in which there are fewer fixed, pre-aesthetic forms to distract the novice. For the individual painting is, as its place in the museum testifies, a thing in its own right, a valued and valuable something-out-there composed of material, of stuff, that as a medium is unambiguous. But it takes considerable effort and skill on the part of the poet, as well as a knowing receptivity on the part of the reader, to allow the poem to take on a similar "feel."

At their best, though, poets seek to remedy the a priori deficiencies of language as an aesthetic medium by undoing its prior meanings and by conferring something like a bodily substance upon it, however their actions violate the way in which language is used to functioning. As Sigurd Burckhardt puts it, the poet must "drive a wedge between words and their meanings" to keep us drawn to the words themselves as things, "and thereby inhibit our all too ready flight from them to the things they point to."[8] It is a making-strange of language, what Russian formalists used to call "defamiliarization" or what Michael Riffaterre calls "ungrammaticality."[9] The fact that critics like Burckhardt or Riffaterre work so effectively with puns and ambiguities (in which "many meanings can have *one word*"[10]) is a likely consequence of this effort to see words in poetry as taking on material substance. For poets to transform phonetic coincidence into semantic inevitability is for them to rivet our attention upon the words themselves as sensory entities, converting words into a proper medium in spite of themselves.

So one striking manifestation of language considered as a proper aesthetic medium is the manipulation of the sounds of words as sensory matter. Here would seem to be a justification for the apparently perverse willingness of so many poets for so long to restrict themselves within severe patterns of meter and rhyme. Surely this is an extreme gesture to their need to "drive a wedge between words and their meanings," to call attention to words as sensory entities. For these poets words thus become manipulable elements, displaying an "aesthetic surface" like that of the plastic media,[11] thus emphasizing their sensory character, calling our attention to their substance as self-sufficient things instead of to their transparency as would-be

---

[8]"The Poet as Fool and Priest: A Discourse on Method," *Shakespearean Meanings* (Princeton: Princeton University Press, 1968), p. 24.

[9]Riffaterre, *Semiotics of Poetry* (Bloomington: Indiana University Press, 1978). "Ungrammaticality" is for him a central concept. Defined on p. 2, it recurs throughout the book.

[10]Burckhardt, *op. cit.*, p. 32.

[11]I take the phrase from D. W. Prall, who uses it to characterize those media—such as we find in the plastic arts or music—that are defined by an intrinsic, discriminable, sensory order. See his "The Elements of Aesthetic Surface in General," *Aesthetic Judgment* (New York: Thomas Y. Crowell, 1929), especially pp. 57–75. In accordance with the usual tradition in aesthetics, he does not find the verbal arts conducive to his analysis of "surface." After excluding them from the above discussion, he treats the problem of verse on pp. 166–73.

pointers. Words thus manipulated demand that we treat them as an aesthetic medium and not as we do in routine discourse, that we attend them rather than going through them once we have deciphered their code; each formal group of them wants to be seen centripetally rather than centrifugally, as a filled and present center and not as one that has been emptied out and turned into an absence. We pretty nearly can heft them and, consequently, come to pay tribute to their innate powers that overwhelm the distance and the arbitrary relation between signifier and signified that governs the normal use of language. Far from arbitrary, they persuade us of their corporeal indispensability.

In elite literary works, I would argue, an "illusion" of presence—of here-and-now-ness—together with the self-reference that follows from that sense of illusionary presence, arises out of what begins as ordinary words and apparently ordinary sentences on the page. As Ernst Gombrich has taught us, this is probably no more or less an illusion than that imposed upon us by the self-consciously make-believe presence we have in the plastic arts. On these grounds literary theorists have found a way to allow their art to partake of the elite character of terminal presence that the post-Kantian aesthetic and our culture have provided for the painting or the sculpture. Of course, though I have concentrated on language, there are other than purely linguistic ways to achieve the effect of physical presence in literature. We become more aware of them as we move from lyric poetry to the other major literary genres. In the drama, for example, there are the realities (though only illusionary realities) of the spatial relations on the stage, the realities that led Lessing to think of the play as a "moving picture." As writers of verse manipulate their medium, creating the illusions that convert words into things, so dramatists—simply by the make-believe that is their primary given—create the illusion that converts the action of characters onstage into "real life" happenings. Or novelists seek the illusion that converts fictions into histories or biographies (or, if in the first person, into autobiographies or journals). Though we retain our awareness that it is an illusion, an act of make-believe, a fiction, we also entertain it as an illusion of a real happening; this is the lingering truth behind the mimetic doctrine in literary criticism. But the work must not be permitted to dissolve into that real happening; we must remember that it is merely mimetic, an illusion that is conscious of itself, that has its own terminal presence—all this thanks to the author's manipulations, which keep us formally rooted in it.

We see, then, that more than the words themselves can serve as the literary medium, which is to be worked into the illusion of a presence analogous to what can be more immediately achieved in the plastic arts. In the language arts anything will serve as a medium that an author can distort from its usual non-aesthetic way of functioning into the peculiar function the work requires. The essence of the medium for authors is its capacity to sponsor deviations under authorial guidance; and, as they make these deviations internally purposive within their special constructs, they demonstrate their powers to convert another commonplace aspect of language or its usual references into their aesthetic medium. Whether it is language itself, or the space (real space and stage space) in the drama, or the imagined space in which events and characters interact in life and narrative, the literary artist can manipulate these into that strangely duplicitous ontology that literary illusions enjoy, allowing us to see them both as mimetic of the world's terms and as unremovably here on their own terms. And that is not very different, after all, from the ambiguous reality we attribute to the representational painting or sculpture, once we understand them to be illusions in Gombrich's sense.

The history of this aesthetic tradition, with the obvious advantages in it (and in our culture's preferences) enjoyed by the material arts that occupy space, would seem to give to poets—in comparison to plastic artists—the more difficult task and cast them in a disadvantaged role as, like other artists, they fight to achieve presence for their created objects. Surely, we can think of the poem as an object, analogous to a painting or sculpture, only by a metaphorical stretch of the imagination. And the fact that poets must undo the way language operates in order to make it operate their way, as a medium, seems to double their difficulties—especially since poets cannot, even in the end, count on an audience that is prepared to undo their own non-poetic reading habits to cultivate the poem's totality. Nevertheless, it can be argued that the successful poet can make the most of these handicaps, converting the deficiencies of language as a medium into unique advantages. We have worried here about the ambiguities of language as a medium: words are at once empty signifiers, part of a pre-arranged, conventional code that poets inherit; and words are remade by poets, who persuade us to discover and concentrate upon a fullness that they force within words. On another level, the poet's fiction reminds us of the world it imitates, and it creates a free-standing make-believe world of its own. Both verbal functions and both worlds must be sustained by the poem, and by us as we read it, at the same time. But these very ambiguities open special opportunities for the literary work of art, allowing it to embrace a now-you-see-it-now-you-don't duplicity that gives it a richness and complexity that less ambiguous arts would find hard to match. What I am suggesting is that the literary arts, being forced to find their aesthetic justification on grounds that assimilate them to the material and spatial arts, can make those grounds peculiarly their own and make the word the most effective of media by straining it to exceed its conventional properties.

But no one should be more aware of the special character of literary language than literary critics, who are obliged to use their own language to describe and interpret the language of the poem. As critics use language their own way, they must respect the difference between that way and the poets' use of language as their medium, or else critics will be unjust to the poem and submerge it within their own egos. It is obvious for critics of the arts other than literature (like the plastic arts) that the language of their criticism is utterly different from the language (if we may metaphorically call it that) of the object that gives rise to criticism. Literary critics may be seduced, perhaps by their arrogance, into being less aware of the great difference between their criticism and its object. (I take up the consequences of such arrogance as the subject of my second lecture, to which this discussion may serve as an introduction.) My argument has been meant to persuade you that, within the terms of the aesthetic tradition I have been examining, words, in literary criticism, can be just as radically distant from words in a poem as words, in criticism of the plastic arts, are from "made things." For we have been observing that a poem too is a "made thing": it has remade the language that makes it up, turning it into a true medium that gives its construct the illusion of being a thing like other art objects.

Yet our continuing awareness of the empty transparency of words—their mere airiness—behind the illusion of their bodily presence reminds us of how fabricated (and wilfully self-deceptive) our experience of the poem is. All this literary critics, fabricating their own fictions, must seek to capture, though not by mistaking their language for the poem's. If it is true that literary criticism is more advanced than criticism of the arts, it is not because literary critics share a common medium with poets. Indeed, it is the fact that critics do not that might well make literary criticism the messier, since—as I shall point out in my second lecture—the critics may well confuse the poets' instrument with their own.

If literary critics spend their time dealing with the doubleness of words in poetry (the before and after of words, as old meanings take on the character of new things), critics of the plastic arts can deal directly with new things themselves—especially when they deal with non-representational art. It is true that in representational art, critics with iconographic interests also are concerned with a doubleness, converting apparent imitation into radical construction, old objects into new illusions. In this practice they may seem less distant from literary critics, as Gombrich might well argue, since he claims an illusionism in all the arts that turns all signs—natural and arbitrary—equally into conventional signs. But the critics of non-representational art would apparently go directly to the constructed thing itself, the art object before them without a past that it has transformed. The critics of representational art cannot join the critics of non-representational art, but must share the literary critics' more mediated approach, sharing also their view of the medium as doubled, as having both a before and an after, both a givenness and a constructedness. From the perspective of such critics, and of the objects they admire, it is likely that one would lament the thinning of human experience in works produced by an arbitrary constructivism for its own sake. Non-representational works would thus be seen as sponsored by an anti-humanistic extreme that has too narrow a conception of that internal purposiveness that symbolizes the artist's imposition of form.

But now we are back to the Kantian aesthetic and to the special object—and our idolatry of it—to which it gave rise. In turning, here at the end, to the critic's activity, I have pointed out that it is, in this tradition, to be wholly directed by its need to be an adequate hand-maid to the work of art, which is criticism's only excuse for existence. (This is, as I have suggested, a notion we shall see placed in severe jeopardy in my next lecture.) Now that we have tended carefully to the aesthetic that created the isolated realm of precious objects, we should move on to the leveling impulse that has sought to devaluate them and bring them down to the rest of our objects. It was, of course, the epithet "aesthetic" that had to be denied. The means of denial was the demystification of the category "aesthetic": what was required was the argument that the elitist claim of disinterested aesthetic value was a mask for a very interested claim of a less glorious sort. Kant's theory, I remember a distinguished commentator on the arts saying at a recent public meeting of art scholars, not only was "nonsense," but was an "unmitigated disaster" for the history of art.[12] It was the notion of aesthetic value and the segregation of the elite group of art objects that the speaker had in mind as nonsensical and disastrous.

As I have suggested from the start, in my discussion of the social accompaniments of Kant's aesthetic, it has had some unfortunate economic and political effects. Or is it that the aesthetic was (as has been suggested) a fraud, a deception to cover the real and utterly interested motives, so that the economic and political are not effects but causes? Something of this sort is what the demystifiers of the aesthetic and its companion elite want to claim. They would be quick to point out that, in speaking of the precious objects that fill our museums, we seem to be using the word "precious" with some ambiguity. Everything we have traced from Kant's aesthetic argues for an intrinsic aesthetic value derived from its own system of internal relations, and yet the word "value" is also ambiguous, or is at least metaphorical, with the source of the metaphor casting some suspicion on the purity of the aesthetic character of its appeal to us. The work's marketplace value, it can be argued, is supposed to be founded on its aesthetic value. And a profession of connoisseurship has sprung up to distinguish works of value and help us make a definitive "assessment." (The marketplace puns persist and are significant.)

One need hardly be a Marxist to recognize something less than total disinterest in an aesthetic value that can have such worldly consequences. Indeed, an avid "interest" shows itself everywhere. For example, the loot that was liberated for the museums of London and

[12]David Antin, speaking as chairperson of the panel on "The Problems of Criticism," at the College Art Association convention in Los Angeles, in February 1977.

22

Paris or was shipped, after increasingly great expenditures, to the museums of the New World, seems evident testimony of the questionable purity of values that, presenting themselves as aesthetic, are so costly as well. Such observations suggest to the skeptical that the objects being worshipped in the museums are indeed precious in more than spiritual ways and that their material reality is indispensable, not to their aesthetic appeal, but to the acquisitive instincts of those who would possess them. This, of course, is to put the entire aesthetic realm into question, reducing it to a self-deceptive rationalization of our coarser bourgeois impulses. The precious objects are indeed elite objects, of the absolutely highest class, their status—as with other social classes—measured in a scheme of quantifiable value. Their intrinsic worth (again the marketplace pun) is then no more stable than the extrinsic worth placed upon them. They no more deserve their high state than the social class that every egalitarian revolution properly aims at. Such a view of our profoundly cherished masterworks, and the demystification of them that it claims, must turn our pious approach to the aesthetic realm into nothing more than a fetish, and a vulgar one at that. [13]

This anti-elitist assault cannot stop short of literature, even though—as we have seen at some length—literature is surely innocent of claiming a value that is rooted in an expensive object. Still the attack on the aesthetic and the notion of a segregated elite must include literature, which has managed to accommodate itself to the aesthetic in ways that we have examined. Literature, I suppose, could be seen as a displacement (in Freud's sense) of the fraudulent aesthetic that disguises its acquisitive instincts and its attachment to commodities. What would be a more self-convincing disguise than to have a kind of art object that must wander free of a material embodiment and remain without worldly value? How could one more convincingly demonstrate the spiritual authority of the aesthetic realm and the irrelevance of the worldly by-products of objects that do have monetary worth? Of course, instead of following so strained and involute—indeed so inverted—an argument, we may prefer simply to believe that, far from

---

[13] I am, of course, using the notion of "fetishism" after Marx in his opening chapter to *Capital* (1867). The chapter is, appropriately for my purposes, entitled "Commodities."

aiding a disguise, literature, as materially worthless, does indeed serve to make the aesthetic credible on its own terms. But our culture, with its penchant for demystification and for tearing down any notion of elite, even in the realm of man-made objects, may well be against us. I shall examine the state and the consequences of this anti-elitism in the arts in my final lecture. We shall find that, in the eagerness to put arts on the level, it is not simply that the museums have lost their walls; it is that the world itself has become the "museum without walls."

PLATE 3   Object ⟩ Subject

2. LITERARY CRITICISM: A PRIMARY OR A SECONDARY ART?

In this second lecture I concentrate upon criticism and its special role in the leveling of the literary art, returning to my more general discussion of the arts in my final lecture. Criticism is, obviously, the discourse traditionally used to determine the elite-making or the leveling of the arts. But in recent times, which have brought the leveling of the arts, criticism—and especially literary criticism—has taken advantage of the opportunity to expand its own role. Some have claimed it to be no less an art than the poetry to which it is to minister. Or, rather, they may be claiming that poetry is to sink into the general pool of writing of which criticism is another—and an equal—example. We shall see, since I want here to examine the special case of recent criticism—its attitudes both to literature and to itself.

Until a decade or so ago we would not seriously have doubted that the fundamental task of literary criticism was to interpret works of "imaginative literature," thereby making them available to their culture, and to subject them to the constant revaluations that, by arranging and rearranging the make-up of a literary canon, would supervise a culture's literary taste. In accordance with this historically sanctioned task, most literary critics have until recently taken for granted the commonplace that their verbal artifact finds its starting point where another verbal artifact has left off, and that the latter is prior both temporally and authoritatively to what they write *about* it. Whatever their feelings about the referentiality of the originally creative work of literature itself, they have seemed to accept the obvious fact of the intended referentiality of their own work of interpretation and judgment. Whatever their epistemology in aesthetics, they have appeared as naive realists in relating their own texts to the master text. For they mutely acknowledged that original work as the ground and the very reason for their own, thereby promising us some attempt at fidelity to their object and inviting us to judge the work of criticism, at least in part, in accordance with the fidelity it achieves.

Now there are other critics writing on many of the same works, within a Western tradition that—with whatever changes become necessary from time to time—has established its restricted canon of original works deserving such critical treatment. Consequently, the individual critic has likely proceeded in a way that recognizes not only the fixed and absolute priority of the original work, but also the subsequent—if conditional—priority of earlier critical works, which could have their authority challenged by the newer critic even if their temporal precedence is unquestioned. Each critic can, in other words, argue with received interpretations and evaluations of individual works and the groups of works we call movements, beginning each critical text where the others have left off in dealing with the original master text. Yet each critic begins—as, presumably, did the others previously—by assuming that original authority against which the new work must be measured as it challenges its earlier (and later) rivals. But it is not to challenge or threaten to supplant or supersede that original, which, interpreted this way or that by this critic or others, will continue to stand and to authorize further critics. In this circular way the original is the ultimate judge of those whose work was intended to furnish a rationalization for our judgment of that original.

Critics are thus seen as the intermediaries between the original work and its culture, seeking to speak out for a work that, for all it says, must—like Keats' urn—be silent about its own meaning. That is, the critic's is a twice-told tale: he or she tells a tale that, already told, can say no more in its own behalf. But the critic's is a second telling, never a first. Trying to make manifest all that is potentially locked in the work, the critic would allow it to "perform" itself thoroughly for the audience being created for it by this act of criticism. So critics interpret and—implicitly or explicitly—evaluate, helping to improve the taste of their culture by their arguments, which can corroborate the place a work has in the elite canon of works or can claim a place in the canon for a work wrongly excluded or, more rarely, can seek to deflate a highly received opinion of a work in order to remove it from the canon. For a work to be elevated into the canon is for it—almost literally—to be canonized.

Always, within such a conception of the nature and function of literary criticism, subsequent readers and critics judge the work of the critic and compare it to others by invoking that ultimate authority of the primary work, next to which all works are secondary. This is again to say that the critic's work of judgment is finally to be judged by the work he or she is presumably judging (or at least by our own version of that original work, a version that must, of course, itself come to be judged by it). The history of criticism may thus be seen as celebrating the sacred mystery that permeates the circle of both interpretation and judgment, a circle presumably made "just" by being made to end where it began—with the authority of the work itself.

I have deliberately overstated the case, using my rhetoric to urge the presence of a fetishizing motive for criticism as commentary on a sacred text, as allegory for an ultimately unspeakable symbol. In this way I point up my observation that, however sophisticated critics have been about the nature of the poetic discourse they seek to unlock for us (however skeptical about its relation to *its* reality), they remain—at least to the extent they mean to be faithful—committed to a naive realism concerning the relation of their own discourse to its object. If my observation is valid, it may be no rhetorical exaggeration for my language to emphasize the fetishization of the original works and the sanctified canon made up of them.

This fidelity to a reified object is a consequence to be expected, given the assumptions of the usual notion of criticism in our history, although it is obvious that most critics who share these assumptions are hardly prepared to push them explicitly to such idolatrous extremes. Further, if such are the almost automatic assumptions made by critics as they have addressed their role as interpretive and judgmental mediators acting in behalf of literary works for their culture, it is also the case that individual critics have frequently acted in accordance with lines less cleanly demarcated between creative and critical functions. An obvious example is Matthew Arnold, who—in his central essay, "The Function of Criticism at the Present Time" (1864)—may have distinguished clearly enough between poetry and criticism, but who did so largely in order to allow criticism to appropriate some of the creative power normally granted poetry.[1] In the course of his argument he further proceeds to free criticism from a referential

---

[1] I treat Arnold's expansion of the domain of criticism beyond the criticism of literary works in my essay, "The Critical Legacy of Matthew Arnold; or, the Strange Brotherhood of T. S. Eliot, I. A. Richards, and Northrop Frye," *Southern Review,* 5 (1969), pp. 457–74. (Reprinted in *Poetic Presence and Illusion: Essays in Critical History and Theory* [Baltimore: Johns Hopkins University Press, 1979], pp. 92–107.)

obligation to poems by enlarging the domain of the word "criticism" from strictly literary criticism (that is, the criticism of literary works) to the general criticism of human and social problems that constitutes the world of ideas. And it becomes clear here and in other of his writings that this general promulgation of "the best that has been thought and said in the world" by poetry and criticism alike becomes, in the broadest sense, the indivisible realm of literature. As an early version of *"écriture,"* such a notion clearly entails the loss of distinction between poetry (as self-conscious fiction-making) and its fellow discourses more directly concerned with communicating ideas, so that the door has been opened to putting the poem and the critical discourse about it at the same level of creativity, essentially blurring the distinction between them. Arnold hardly meant to dethrone poetry from its special role in culture (see, for example, his idolatrous claims in "The Study of Poetry" about poetry's "high destinies" and "immense" future as a surrogate religion), but implicit in the creative power he gave to criticism to generate ideas is a leveling of discourse that could serve to undermine the limited notion of criticism as a secondary art serving the primary art of poetry, held aloft as its proper subject and justification.

Or one may cite, as another example of critics who seem to blur the dividing line between poetic and critical discourse, the willed self-indulgence of critical impressionism. Whether we speak of the free, subjective projections sponsored (late in the last century and early in this one) by the call to "creative criticism" or of the more recent merger of the critic's and the poet's subjectivities in the Geneva School "critics of consciousness," we seem to be licensing in the critic an independence of voice that may seem to challenge the priority of the poem as the critic's "object," which, I have suggested, our critical tradition has taken for granted. But even as liberating a suggestion as Georges Poulet's that criticism is "literature about literature" acknowledges an about-ness in the critic's obligation, so that criticism, though literature, is clearly a second-order literature and hence derivative. However such criticism strays over the line toward poetry, it is hardly being granted an independent authority as an autonomous function.

Nevertheless, in contrast to occasional moods that have impelled some critics during the past century and a half toward usurpation of the poet's role, the more modest assumptions about the critic's role—like those I have outlined above—generally held sway until the revolutionary conceptions of criticism in the last decade or so. Indeed, during the days of the largely unquestioned supremacy of the New Criticism, the critics' role as faithful vassals to the poem achieved its strongest assertion: the poetic "object" was to be treated as the critics' idol, as the sole justification of their joyfully acknowledged subsidiary existence. Of course, the work was to be taken as totally interpretable, so that each critic was to have arrogance enough to offer the ultimate key to interpretation, but always—so the oath of fidelity went—in the service of each master text, from which it was an obligation to keep personal interests distinct. In the flurry of interpretations and reinterpretations—with the consequent evaluations and revaluations—all mystery was to be discursively exposed in a burst of hermeneutic hubris such as criticism had probably never known. And it may very well have been this excess that prepared the way for the inversion that the very concept of criticism as a serving art has undergone in recent years. I may in my turn have to suggest that the claim to critical autonomy—with its denial of priority to literature—is itself excessive.

Several varieties of criticism that are currently fashionable reveal an assumption that the critical tradition I have been describing must find shocking in its self-assertiveness, even if it has today become a commonplace: that the critical work and the poem, which is its presumed object, are of the same order of creativity; that, despite our intuitive sense of which comes first, both may claim an equal priority. In other words, criticism, no less than what we usually think of as "imaginative literature," is a primary art, and the writing of criticism a primary act. In speaking of "criticism" here, I am not using the word in the broad Arnoldian sense, which would include all apparently non-fictional prose and could be applied to the large groups of writers—like Montaigne, Pascal, Rousseau, Marx, Nietzsche, or Arnold himself—whose work these days seems so attractively available for critical study. I shall not in this essay (though I do elsewhere)[2] argue whether or not that sort of criticism in the broad sense should be treated as imaginative

---

[2]In "Literature vs. *Ecriture*: Constructions and Deconstructions in Recent Critical Theory," *Studies in the Literary Imagination,* 12 (1979), pp. 1–17. (Reprinted in *Poetic Presence and Illusion,* pp. 169–87.)

literature of the same order of primacy as what we usually think of as poetry. The case here is more extreme in that I am speaking only of *literary* criticism—criticism which is, presumably, commentary *about* (and, consequently, commentary *after*) literary works, considered singly or in groups. The possible blurring between literature and criticism would, on the face of it, seem harder to justify when the case for criticism has been narrowed to cover only what appears to be literary commentary.

Yet the revolutionary view of criticism that I am here introducing into the argument—though it might see itself free to dwell upon general non-poetic discourse as well as poetry—would hardly settle for anything less than primacy even for itself as a work of explicitly literary criticism, though it appears to spring from the stimulus of other works. We can look, for example, at the complaint of Edward Said, who argues for this revolutionary concept of criticism, a criticism that for him shares the repetitive character of all literature. He is arguing here against the traditional notion of criticism:

> For in a very deep way, critical discourse is still ensnared by a simplistic opposition between originality and repetition, in which all literary texts worth studying are given the former classification, the latter being logically confined mainly to criticism and to what isn't worth studying. I believe such schemata to be hopelessly paralyzing. They mistake the regularity of most literary production for originality, while insisting that the relation between "literature" and criticism is one of original to secondary; moreover, they overlook, in both traditional and modern literature, the profoundly constitutive use of repetition—as motif, device, epistemology, and ontology.[3]

Where repetition is everywhere, then all work is a coming-after, and originality—like the very notion of origins—is a myth. This notion reminds us that I may have put the matter wrongly by seeing recent criticism as fighting to claim poetry's primacy for itself; what I should rather have suggested is that criticism can accept a secondary status so long as it shares that status with literature. If there is no primacy in criticism, it is because there is no literal primacy in discourse at all; thus there is no *less* primacy in criticism than in "literature."

Let me suggest four related ways in which recent critical attitudes

[3]Edward Said, "Roads Taken and Not Taken in Contemporary Criticism," in *Directions for Criticism: Structuralism and Its Alternatives,* ed. Murray Krieger and L. S. Dembo (Madison: University of Wisconsin Press, 1977), p. 50.

encourage such a notion of equal primacy (or non-primacy) for criticism to become an almost automatic presupposition in some quarters these days. To begin with, the notion may be seen as a consequence of the acknowledgment, produced by epistemological candor, that the critics' pretension to deal "objectively" with that thing out there (the poem) that stands outside their discourse, having preexisted it, is belied by the reflexive nature of their activity. Critics have for some time been readier than they used to be to confront the radical subjectivity that underlies their sincerest efforts at disinterested analysis and appraisal.[4] Their desire to be responsive to controls (in the object) that they claim to discover—and that they seek to persuade others to discover with them—is no longer permitted to hide the fact that they have projected the controls out of their experience with the poem. So criticism is now confessed to be—and to have always been—a rewriting of the object in the critics' own terms, and thus in effect the creation of a new object, or rather of a projection that the critic then treats as if it were the discovered object. Whatever the hopes for fidelity, the poem the critic is faithful to is in the end his or her own. Once this element of narcissistic reduction is seen as paramount, the confessional nature of the critical act and product is itself confessed to. The poem itself, reduced to a minimal stimulus, becomes—in both senses of the word—a mere "pretext." And critical discourse can be elevated into the primary text itself.

A second justification of criticism as a primary art, perhaps another version of the first, is urged by those theorists who put all forms of writing on the same footing as created fictions, each of them similarly projected out of an author's tropes as well as out of narrative structures. They would reject any distinction between those—like poems—that self-consciously intend to be fictions only and those— like criticism—that seem to intend to refer, with a claim to accuracy with which one can agree or disagree, to other discourse.[5] So viewed (and I think especially of Hayden White as viewing it this way), criticism—plotted in accordance with the fiction that it depends on a

---

[4]See, as an example, my *Theory of Criticism: A Tradition and Its System* (Baltimore: Johns Hopkins University Press, 1976), Chap. 3.

[5]For example, see Hayden White, "Introduction: Tropology, Discourse, and the Modes of Human Consciousness," *Tropics of Discourse: Essays in Cultural Criticism* (Baltimore: Johns Hopkins University Press, 1978).

prior fiction—is primary as both art and act in the sense that all acts, as art—that is, as texts—are equally primary.

This concept can be pressed toward a third, also derived from the denial of the apparent intentions of all texts, in which texts are reduced to being rationalizations of the author's "will to power" or "political unconscious." Theorists, like Edward Said and Fredric Jameson, in making this claim are not satisfied with stopping the deconstructive process once the assumed stable meanings of the text have been changed into a fictional and tropological play among signifiers; they rather pursue that process beyond all texts—until textual pretensions are traced back to the political or psychological motive that puts the text forward as an insidious verbal disguise. For these critics, whether they derive from Marx or Nietzsche or Freud, there is no innocent text, no disinterestedness in its production or reception: instead, though the text offers itself and its fiction as all there is, the author means to use it to manipulate the actual world, to imperialize the world one way only. And poems are no different from criticism in offering themselves for reduction to this subterranean intent.

From these three notions a fourth can be derived: that all writings, like their writers, are in rivalry with one another.[6] As Harold Bloom would have it, poets are seen as competing with their predecessors no more than critics compete with their poet-subjects and with earlier critics of those poets: each work struggles against the fact of time—of the priority of others—to establish its own claim to primacy. All texts, poems and critical works alike, feed on one another, so that—from this perspective—no text is actually primary. The intertextuality all texts share is their ego-driven reason for being and assures the lack of hierarchy or priority among their claims, as these are given status by the theorist.

These and probably other arguments are being advanced for the granting of the poet's license to the critic. In view of the idiosyncratic freedoms—either of interpretation or of judgment—taken by critics throughout the history of their discipline and specially bestowed upon them recently, is it stubborn and naive to insist that such defenses of criticism's primacy and independence are excessive? Is it, in other

[6]The obvious example is Harold Bloom. Among his recent books, see especially *The Anxiety of Influence* (New York: Oxford University Press, 1973) and *The Map of Misreading* (New York: Oxford University Press, 1975).

words, merely unrealistic to refuse to sanction in theory what in fact criticism is so often doing?

Successful critical movements, looked at from some distance, pretty generally can be seen as following a similar pattern of development as each arises, moves toward dominance, and then—through over-expansion—declines in favor of the rival movement that succeeds it, and retraces the pattern. Indeed, the history of a critical doctrine seems more political than intrinsically theoretical in character. The stages each movement goes through in defense of its doctrine reflect its imperialistic motive and its increasing subjugation of literary works to its needs, the subduing of them in order to appropriate from them what it must have in order to thrive.

The movement begins, modestly enough, out of the desire to ac-count for literary works, or certain aspects of literary works, that existing criticism either neglects or accounts for inadequately (as it seems to those dissatisfied enough to go a new way). These new proponents may even have the innocent belief that their theoretical quest is honestly empirical: there stand some works in the literary corpus, there are the received critical notions that either ignore them or do not do right by them, and here is the corrective to be applied in the interest of critical justice. As a consequence, the new movement implicitly seeks a reordering of the literary canon, with the works added that the movement is being invented to account for.[7]

As the new doctrine succeeds in drawing critics to its theoretical perspective, it naturally becomes bolder; or, rather, its new adherents, with the zeal of converts, make claims more grandiose than its less confident inventors would have dared. What had perhaps begun as a modest desire to ask—on a live-and-let-live basis—that some con-sideration be given to literary values different from those currently favored, for less favored works to join more favored ones in the literary canon, gradually is transformed into the demand that we drop those literary works that the now superseded movement had over-

---

[7]This is not to suggest that authors or works necessarily displace one another. Obviously there are some that are inevitables, that must stay in the canon and be accounted for regardless of the peculiar interests of each movement. But in each case these stay, in effect, as different authors or works serving different canonical needs. We have only to recall the new (and sometimes strange) Shakespeare presented by each revolution in taste and theoretical assumptions. The canon has been redone even when many of the names remain the same.

rated (at least from the point of view of the newly reigning movement). This development toward exclusivity may be viewed as an acknowledgment of the obvious consequences that the theory sponsoring the newly dominant doctrine has carried within itself all along. Its founders may have been incapable of freeing themselves altogether from the now obsolete notions, so that they were too cautious in their exclusions. Only with the second-generation proponents can the new doctrine succeed in purifying itself and reordering literary history in order to reflect its values.

Only in the final stage of the ascendancy of the movement can its imperialistic cravings achieve full satisfaction. What is reached is a new universalism of taste, but only on the terms of the doctrine. Those large numbers of literary works excluded from the canon, in the flush of the doctrine's success in promoting its own favorites, are now readmitted, though they have now been subjected to re-readings that make them seem very much like the doctrine's own favorites. The works have, in effect, been rewritten (that is, interpreted in ways different from earlier rewritings), have been turned into just the sort of works the doctrine has been admiring, and these works are now forced to serve as supporting members of a canon primarily constituted by the reigning doctrine's original favorites. As the second stage rewrote the history of the literature, creating a canon of new heroes while excluding many of the old ones, this final stage rewrites the individual works in order to make them all eligible for a newly expanded, all-inclusive canon, though the model that in the end they all resemble is that furnished by those heroes created in the second stage. The rising, exclusivistic fervor of the young establishmentarian has relaxed into the catholicity of the mature imperialist.

If we may, for purposes of a fable, reduce a movement to a single person, his career might run as follows: a critical reformer begins by wanting only to deal with a small group of poems which, treated unjustly by predecessors and contemporaries, stands in need of what his peculiar theory can do for it. Then, bolstered by his "discoveries" about the poems, he calls for their upward revaluation, but without casting aspersions on their more cherished rivals. However, ambition drives him: moving outward from the same principles, he sees other poems, formerly highly valued according to principles outmoded by his, as falling short. And he remodels the tradition to reflect *his* ideal poem, leaving out the others. Finally he moves beyond such parochialism: upon reexamination, he finds in the devalued poems the very characteristics his ideal poems have (presumably) taught him to treasure. Wherever he looks, he sees that same poem and wonders at the large number of splendid works in our tradition, and at the sameness of their splendor. Alas, he has ceased to be interesting and is ready to be replaced (and rejected) by the next reformer (and one is always waiting at such turns in our critical history).

Even such a simple-minded parody of what happens seems not altogether at variance with how movements rise and fall and succeed one another.[8] As just one example, if we think briefly (and perhaps superficially) about the history of the New Criticism and its culmination in the work of Cleanth Brooks, we can find traces of this pattern. In the writings of those we think of either as forerunners of the New Criticism or as early New Critics, we find the attempt to elevate a kind of poetry that they thought to be undervalued by their predecessors and contemporaries. For example, the ground-breaking review by T. S. Eliot of the Grierson anthology ("The Metaphysical Poets," 1921) tries to rescue several poets from critical neglect or charges of eccentricity in order to persuade the reader to acknowledge that they "are in the direct current of English poetry."[9] And while there is a disparagement of some who have been accepted as major poets, the tone is clearly too tentative and the thinking too seminal to permit our finding in the essay a new order of values to be accorded to the varieties of English poetry. But the beginnings are there, to be developed by those who will follow to consolidate the claim.

[8]One may, of course, overemphasize the revolutionary character of each new movement and thus overlook its familial relation—as rebellious son to father—to the tired movement it supplants. A close examination reveals a complexity of motive and response made familiar to us by Harold Bloom. Thus, despite what may seem to be the violence of its reaction, the new movement is doomed, in spite of its best efforts, to carry the rejected one on its back as it proceeds to undo it. For it also *re*does that movement, repeating, at least, the exclusivity of its claim to dominance. So, even when substantive positions are inverted into negation, there may be an echo of what was to have been reformed. The rejected predecessor comes also to be seen, somehow, as a precursor. Nevertheless, despite the workings of such subtle qualifications of motive and direction, I would maintain that—viewed from the broad historical perspective—the pattern of the rise and fall of movements, and the displacement of one by the next, is pretty much as I am describing it here.

[9]Eliot, "The Metaphysical Poets," *Selected Essays,* new ed. (New York: Harcourt Brace & Co., 1950), p. 250.

The newly proclaimed heroes of this criticism are poems in which certain developments of metaphor and complex plays of tone are prominent. Throughout the thirties, critics like John Crowe Ransom and Allen Tate pressed Eliot's suggestions forward and applied them in ways that began to propose new orderings of poetic value, although their gentility kept them from enlarging their conclusions until they pronounced a theoretical manifesto. It was left to Cleanth Brooks to fulfill the daring implicit in Eliot's early work and becoming more and more explicit in the work of Ransom and Tate. The youthful boldness of *Modern Poetry and the Tradition* (1939) is gathered up in the concluding chapter, "Notes for a Revised History of English Poetry." The poets of early seventeenth-century wit become the major poets of our history, and the most importantly influential too, since it is they who stand behind the poetry of Eliot, Yeats, Auden, and the rest, who after all this time have finally come along to pick up the essential (which is to say, the most highly valued) English poetic tradition. And between the two groups most of the work is now seen as clearly inferior, with a few exceptional poets or a few exceptional moments in poets otherwise faulty, though these are the great names that have filled our anthologies. After such a systematizing of the claims of the movement, Ransom—perhaps infected by Brooks' daring—can now step in to consolidate the movement by giving it its name with his book, *The New Criticism* (1941).

But the inevitable final imperialistic thrust is to follow. When Brooks publishes *The Well Wrought Urn* (1947), he brings together mainly essays that salvage poems from even the least likely of those poets earlier expelled from the pantheon (Milton, Pope, Gray, Wordsworth, and even Tennyson). But if they were wrongly excluded before, it is only because—on closer look—one now can find in their work many of the attributes that accounted for the praise of the favorites in the revisionist history of English poetry. So the poems of this newly reabsorbed group seem more and more to resemble those of Donne and the others, as these latter have been read by New Critics. Thus it is a useful tactic for Brooks also to include in this book a few chapters devoted to poems more obviously in the New Critical orthodoxy (by Donne, Herrick, Keats, and Yeats). What emerges out of this broadened fellowship of poets committed to metaphysical wit is a definition of our best poetry that converts what had been a parochial "school" of poems into a universal formula for all successful poems as speakers of "the language of paradox." The takeover is complete, and secession from the empire is shortly to begin.[10]

Looked at from another perspective, this movement can be seen as occurring not on behalf of a (then) New Criticism, but on behalf of a (then) new poetry. That is, it can be seen as creating the very sort of literary history (based on the very sort of poetic values) it required in order to justify what poetry after Eliot wished to do. In this sense it is a striking example of what Emerson Marks has called "pragmatic poetics," "poetics designed more or less consciously to create a favorable atmosphere not only for the public reception but for the very creation of work in a new idiom."[11] But of course I have meant to broaden that concept here beyond the justification of a new poetic

---

[10]I should mention a subsidiary issue brought to my attention by Professor B. J. Leggett, when these lectures were delivered. It may seem, as he suggested, that the pedagogical diffusion of critical method into a universal way of reading poems, in the textbook efforts of, say, Cleanth Brooks and Robert Penn Warren, engaged the New Critics in a leveling enterprise of their own: the analytical tools for all formalistic reading were placed in everyone's hands. The elite object functioning broadly within a universally literate society—this was precisely the arrangement that the New Critics sought to make possible. The use of education to make even the rarest of poems generally accessible to their culture was a social mission that was surely democratic. Nevertheless, I would see their intent as just the opposite of the leveling I have described in my first lecture and will describe in my third: they seek to raise all of us to the point at which we can appreciate, at their highest, the giants of our literary tradition, to appreciate them *as* giants. If they tried to democratize, through precise and generally available explanation, the capacity to appreciate poems, they wanted universal elevation and not universal reduction. They would have us explain what made the elite poem elite without demystifying it. But, on the other side, one might argue that, in spite of its objectives, the New Critical method had a leveling consequence upon the works because of the uniform way it treated them all, perhaps unintentionally repeating the tendency I observed in the Abbé Batteux of reducing them to a single principle. This may well be the problem of all critical schools that, in their maturity, achieve dominance in the model of the sequence of empires that I am tracing here. (I might add, however, that one might more accurately claim that it was Northrop Frye, the immediate successor to the New Critics, who—again probably in spite of himself—introduced us to the leveling impulse as a demystifying as well as a democratizing impulse, treating poems as displacements and stripping them down to the archetypal formulae rooted in the primal functions of human need and human desire as these define the human imagination. And in more recent years, of course, this impulse has been freely indulged—freely enough to justify the writing of these lectures.)

[11]Emerson R. Marks, "Pragmatic Poetics: Dryden to Valery," *Bucknell Review,* 10 (1962), pp. 213–23.

idiom: what I have been trying to suggest, in agreement with those who view criticism as an independent, creative activity that in reality yields its primacy to no literary work, however "prior," is that all poetics end (or rather begin!) by being pragmatic in their original motive, moving outward toward an imperializing program of universal and systematic assimilation. This program, carried to the extreme contained in the logic of its aesthetic reduction, would dictate how all past poems are to be read and how all future poems are to be written, creating its own fictional narrative as it goes. I could go on to other critical movements—for example those that have followed the New Criticism, whether dominated by Northrop Frye or the "critics of consciousness" or deconstructionist critics—to show the extent to which they arose in response to areas of literature slighted by the New Criticism (or, in the case of some deconstructionist criticism, in response to recent literature that has come after the modernist works that inspired the New Criticism) and then gradually spread their target groups to include works to which these newer methods originally appeared unrelated.

By my proposing such a developmental sequence for critical movements and by thus acknowledging the pragmatic rather than the referential basis of literary criticism, I must appear to be reinforcing the most extravagant claims of those who would deny to criticism any serious responsibility to a literary object, whatever its pretensions. The most extreme self-justification of critical "misreading" as a function of criticism to be lived with and even encouraged—such as Harold Bloom suggests—may seem to be no more than a candid corollary to be drawn from such an analysis as mine. I would thus seem to be using the history of criticism to support the recently growing tendency, which I described earlier, of freeing criticism from any dependence on a prior literary object in order to make it a fully autonomous literary object itself, to be treated as one among equals.

But even if I admit that their innate imperialistic tendencies must always lead critics to rearrange the literary corpus they inherit in order to create the canon their theoretical god requires, I have also suggested that this behavior was often more unconscious than intended, that indeed their would-be empirical mission was what propelled them, as critics, into action. There is, then, this difference between the general failure of critics through history to perform the "secondary" act that it has presumably been their function to perform and the particular commitment of critics under the aegis of this recent license to perform independently. For the first time, I believe, criticism has gone beyond rearranging the canon: in its recent revolutionary mode, criticism has undermined the very principle on which the canon—as a collection of primary works—exists, reconstructing it precisely in order to make a place for itself within it. Though, in the past, criticism has, intentionally or not, altered its object (or, to use a more precise epistemology, recreated it) to serve its needs, it now rejects the notion that it *has* an object, proclaiming itself as a free-ranging, arbitrary subject, an absolute subject that, in effect, can replace the object with itself. Critics thus become true rivals of poets, filling their work with self-conscious reflexivity. They are dependent on prior texts, but no more so than poets are, remaking them into the newness of their own work with the poet's abandon. Critics join the parade of intertextuality as unfettered participants. Like all others, poets and non-poets alike, critics are both doomed to repeat their precursors and free to remake them into themselves, like their precursors doomed to be secondary and free to seek to be primary. Liberated from older criticism's myth of responsibility to an original object, critics can indulge the misreadings authorized by their irresponsibility and reconstitute the body of discourse with their every contribution, fulfilling the task that Eliot had, decades ago, reserved for the talented traditional poet.

What, then, of the role criticism used to dedicate itself—however self-deceptively—to performing? Is it now to be dissolved, or will it not still exist, however unperformed or even unperformable? Because criticism, by its nature, must fail to perform the role except by occasional indirection, should it no longer try, even if only with a self-conscious awareness of its necessary limits, at once epistemological and psychological? The only justification for obliterating the conventional notion of criticism's role is our acknowledgement that, in the new egalitarianizing of writing, there no longer are literary works—no longer a corpus of works to be served, a canon to be continually created and sustained. But I am assuming that there *are* primary works—utterly primary despite their inevitably intertextual character—that deserve not to be abandoned, that historically have stimulated experiences we have found uniquely valuable, experiences that testify to the power of a self-consciously manipulated fiction in a self-consciously manipulated language.

Consequently, I am assuming also that the older and more conventional role of criticism still needs performing. Despite the seductions of critical self-inflation, I must still write in defense of the more modest—if less heroic—conception of criticism as a secondary art. It is an art, surely, and it may seem to share some of its secondary attributes with poetry in their commonly intertextual nature; but it is a second telling of the tale and should accept referential obligations to the poem's first telling. As a limited literary criticism, it must acknowledge the poem as its point of origin, whatever intertextual lines flow into and out of them both. Those readers for whom literary criticism is written retain the right to ask that it try to give readings rather than misreadings, however fated it may be—epistemologically and psychologically—to be trapped within the latter. And the reader, as a rival critic, may quarrel about how far the reading has missed.

What I am suggesting is that the new vogue in criticism, for all its revolutionary attractiveness, is, ultimately, another—though perhaps the most radical—of the many varieties of subjectivism we have seen in the last century. The standard answers given subjectivism by a critical tradition busy with its ongoing work can serve again here. We need the healthy skepticism that reminds us of our egocentric predicament, thereby demystifying the critics' authoritarian claims and their metaphysical ground; but the culture's need to have such claims made—and denied and remade—is not thereby eliminated. We are better off being aware of the pragmatic nature of our critical need, and thus alive to its shaky epistemological foundations, but not if we are led to surrender the referential responsibility of literary commentary and to license critical self-indulgence just because it still asserts itself when we try to rein it in. The critics' instinct for arrogance is compelling enough without being encouraged by the suggestion that they need have no other motive, that their own work need never bow to the superior authority of a text proclaimed as primary by its every word. Critical humility is not a virtue in such over-supply that we should theoretically preclude it. On the contrary, the epistemological reality of the relation of critics to the original text is such that they will always be deluded about any pretense at humility: the subservience of their perspectives to their own needs ensures a self-serving vision, whatever its guise. There can of course be no neutral object out there to serve as monitor, no matter how strait a jacket critics would put on their predilections.

Yet there are times when critics find one another talking about what seems to be the same work. Despite being trapped in our subjectivity, it is hard for us to ignore the partial agreement that dialogue occasionally makes possible among critical readers. If the extent of agreement in critical history seems slight next to the remaining disagreements, the fact that there is *any* agreement is another pragmatic justification for doing what critics ordinarily do and suggests grounds for the phenomenological assumption that there is a common object for critics to dispute about, or at least that the object is not altogether an idiosyncratic one invented to serve their needs. The history of taste can be made to exaggerate evidence about the subjectivity of judgments, despite their most pious professions of disinterestedness, but the disparities would be the more violent if critics began with the assumption that they had fidelity to nothing but their own discourse and the misreadings it cultivates.

The conflict that the Anglo-American critical tradition still wages with the many dominant influences of continental "poststructuralism" has perhaps its most significant consequences (for literary study at least) in this question of the theoretical subservience of criticism to the elite literary text. Acknowledging the strength of the arguments that demystify all that criticism has commonly taken for granted about its operations, criticism yet must clear some ground on which to operate. Still willing to grant the special character of works it has canonized, it feels impelled to retain its function of playing intermediary between these texts and their culture, both making their meaning available and judging them as being worthy of that mediating effort of interpretation.

The interpretive act assumes that the poem is of greater interest and is less self-explanatory as a marshaling of language than the criticism of it is; it assumes that the poem is reflexive and self-deconstructive, so that criticism about it must try—however vainly—to be the referential equivalent of that which cannot speak for itself. But the revolutionary critics who reject such subservience see their own work as possessing the attributes others would confine to poetry, matching or improving upon poetry's self-deconstructive powers. One might even argue that such critics thrive the more as the fortunes of poetry decline. As poems, now denied elite status, dwindle into the common level of writing decreed for them by recent theory, the ambition of criticism can grow proportionately. The classless democracy of texts is encouraged when the nobility of poetry sheds its ennobling characteristics. But now writers of criticism may try to pick those characteristics up, though without running the risk of becoming poets themselves: by seeking to deconstruct that which no longer is granted the capacity to deconstruct itself, critics can hold their own ground while usurping the poets'.

So critics nowadays can be charged with having an interest in the leveling of poetry as discourse, since they see themselves in a stronger position when less distinguished poetry is produced. It is another version of my earlier charge that recent criticism seeks not just to rearrange the corpus, but to put itself into it as at least an equal—indeed, as a first among equals. If it is more than an empty charge, it may account for the fact that some of these critics are supportive of the anti-poetic tendency in much recent poetry, that which would make each poem indistinguishable in kind from all other writing, a text among indiscriminate texts. For the world thus becomes nothing but texts, postmodern texts served by—or rather manipulated by—a postmodern criticism. And only this criticism, providing the deconstructionist's interpretive key to all, turns out to serve as a master text. For it converts earlier works into postmodern texts as well. Here is an extreme example of the course of critical imperialism that I traced earlier.

Culture, consequently, is made to pay a heavy price for the self-aggrandizing impulse of a criticism that would now collapse the world into its reduced vision. We can give full due to those factors in the critical process that inhibit the capacity of critics to close with their object on *its* terms, but in doing so we need not make their work as freely creative as—and no more referential than—a poem. As an example of such concessions made to subjective intrusions while still withholding for criticism a residual function of literary commentary, I would cite my essay, "The Critic as Person and Persona."[12] There I discuss the mutual tensions and distortions in the work of critics produced by the conflicting pressures upon it from the theoretical commitments they represent, from their own private needs as persons, and from the text that confronts them with its own demands. In the case of each confrontation of a poem by a critic, out of the three-way

[12]In *Theory of Criticism*, pp. 38–64.

interaction among persona, person, and text, emerges a vision highly responsive to interests that force the text to serve them, but it is not altogether unresponsive to the text either, and to that extent it can be of some interpretive interest to less skilled readers.

It may thus be possible to profit from the theoretical skepticism that propels the self-conscious awareness of recent criticism without depriving either criticism of its role as literary companion or culture of the interlocutor it requires to keep its most unique accomplishments in language continually functioning for it in their full performance potential. In a critic like Geoffrey Hartman, who seems to share at once the explicative care we have traditionally associated with criticism and the revolutionary daring of the recent self-conscious critical imperialists, we often find the kind of balance I would encourage. A recent essay suggests the most radical claims for criticism in its title ("Crossing Over: Literary Commentary as Literature") and deals with Derrida's *Glas* as a supreme intertextual example of criticism as literature, yet holds back and speaks also for criticism's more traditional function.

> What I am saying then, pedantically enough, and reducing a significant matter to its formal effect, is that literary commentary may cross the line and become as demanding as literature: it is an unpredictable or unstable "genre" that cannot be subordinated, a priori, to its referential or commentating function. Commentary certainly remains one of the defining features, for it is hardly useful to describe as "criticism" an essay that does not review in some way an existing book, show, or documented habit of thought. But the perspectival power of criticism, its strength of recontextualization, must be such that the critical essay should not be considered a supplement to something else. Though the irony described by Lukacs may formally subdue the essay to a given work, a reversal must be possible whereby this "secondary" piece of writing turns out to be "primary."[13]

However far-reaching the literary claims being made here for criticism, there are also concessions enough to maintain the function of the critic as a conserving force.

More than a dozen years ago, in the title essay of *The Play and Place of Criticism*, I tried to balance the needs of critical presumptuousness with those of critical modesty. And although the theoretical issues

[13]Geoffrey Hartman, "Crossing Over: Literary Commentary as Literature," *Comparative Literature,* 28 (1976), p. 265.

seemed very different in those days, I believe the balance I tried to achieve between mutually constraining and even contradictory forces within the critic was not seriously different from what I would urge now, and not seriously different from what I see Hartman as urging. Critics must play, I said, but critics must know their place; indeed, they must somehow make their peace with the injunction to play *within* their place. Although the notion of play would seem to presuppose freedom, somehow the critic's is an almost-but-not-quite-free play (as Derrida uses that phrase), at least according to this injunction. And in that slight qualification placed upon "free play" we find a lingering resistance to the revolutionary criticism of recent deconstructionists by even those who would be most flexible in accommodating older critical practice to what must now be acknowledged about the critic's egocentric predicament.

As play that is not altogether without referential responsibility, criticism becomes variations on a theme. Those variations threaten to form a center of their own, an almost-rival center, but that primary theme arising from criticism's perception *of the work* yet remains the original center that prevents any potential rival from being more than an almost-rival. Though the work must suffer the centrifugal motions that constitute the separate life of criticism, the work remains, ultimately, the origin and the center for the critic's work.

The notion of a play that is not quite free, of independent variations that yet circle a theme, requires the positing of an origin and a center that persist to rivet critics despite their arrogant and even jealous fondness for their own role. The setting forth of such paradoxical functions for the critic, must seem, in view of our recently most fashionable criticism, at once concessive and conservative. It must strike profound disagreement with the post-structuralist will to deconstruct the very claim to any origin or center. The insistence that the poem is the primary text and that criticism—for all its would-be independent flights—is secondary rests on just such a claim to an origin and a center. The contrary insistence on the exclusive and universal operation of intertextuality in discourse must preclude any primary text or such a hierarchy as I suggest and leave all texts leveled in a dynamic field of mutuality.[14]

[14]On the ubiquity of intertextuality and the lack of *origin*ality in any text, one may look almost any place in the recent work of J. Hillis Miller: as just two examples,

In defense of our older critical habits, I can finally do little more than call attention to each critic's innate sense of the superiority of the chosen work, each critic's sense of the work as a mode of discourse different from critical writing. If the critic's arrogance as the present writer (like all writers trying to free themselves from their dependence on past texts) will in any case assert itself, the critic is the better for using conservative theory to curb it. Even if there is a futility in the critic's attempt to get to the work (as if it were available objectively), there are slight—though crucial—differences in degree between what the critic can tell us when the criticism indulges in utterly free play and what the critic can tell us when seeking to range the criticism around the poem. Critics may certainly wish their discursive freedom to be absolute, so that—though no more than critics—they are telling the tale as if for the first time, but it is healthier for them to remember that—as I suggested earlier—theirs is a second telling. Indeed, it is much more than the second, as they join the march of tellers behind the original teller (who *is* the original teller of this tale, if it is a good tale, no matter how rich its sources and how dependent upon them the teller may be). The parade of critics is a long one, and the critic is dependent upon them, as secondary sources, in a way different from the dependence on any primary source and different from the latter's dependence on a tradition of similar primary sources.

The satellites that revolve about a major planet may persuade us of their independent brilliance, but satellites they remain. This is just about the relationship I am urging between criticism and its primary work. There is a different but not totally unallied metaphor in the passage from Plato's *Ion* in which he speaks of the stone of Heraclea. Its wisdom still speaks to us. This passage furnished me with the epigraph for "The Play and Place of Criticism," and it seems especially appropriate as a closing metaphor for what critics do and how it is related to what poets do. Socrates is addressing the rhapsode and praising his excellent commentary about Homer:

. . . there is a divinity moving you, like that contained in the stone which

---

"Walter Pater: A Partial Portrait," *Daedalus* (Winter, 1976), especially p. 105, and "Stevens' Rock and Criticism as Cure, II," *Georgia Review*, 30 (1976), especially p. 334.

Euripides calls a magnet, but which is commonly known as the stone of Heraclea. This stone not only attracts iron rings, but also imparts to them a similar power of attracting other rings; and sometimes you may see a number of pieces of iron and rings suspended from one another so as to form quite a long chain: and all of them derive their power of suspension from the original stone. In like manner the Muse first of all inspires men herself; and from these inspired persons a chain of other persons is suspended, who take the inspiration. . . . Do you know that the spectator is the last of the rings which, as I am saying, derive their power from the original magnet; and the rhapsode like yourself and the actors are intermediate links, and the poet himself is the first link of all?[15]

[15]From the Benjamin Jowett translation of the *Ion.*

PLATE 4   Les Baux 〉 Beaubourg

3. ART AND ARTIFACT
IN A COMMODITY SOCIETY

W̲e have followed at least two
lines of attack on the traditional aesthetic as it applies its theory of
value to the elite object of art. Each addresses itself in its own way to
undermining both the authenticity of the aesthetic and the
application of its theory to works of art. Each seeks to deconstruct
what it sees as a metaphysical claim that disguises quite elementary
desires that seek a high-minded rationalization. One of these, as we
observed in my first lecture, is a path likely to be taken by those who
would resist the idolatry displayed toward material and spatial
objects of art, and the other, as we observed in my second lecture, is a
path likely to be taken by those who would resist the idolatry
displayed toward verbal objects of art. Let us pursue these, one at a
time, to see their consequences for the contemporary criticism of the
arts.

Critics of the plastic arts, especially in their contemporary forms,
must continually be haunted by—and resentful of—the crude realities
of the art market and the influence of that market upon what is or is
not valuable (or, rather, valued) today, and upon what will or will not
be valuable (or valued) tomorrow, as the vagaries of fashion assert
themselves and affect the marketplace value of art in actual dollars. It
may be no wonder, then, that even critics without a Marxist orienta-
tion seek to explode the myth of the aesthetic value of material objects
by showing the value itself to be materialistic. But their demythifying is
easily exposed to the Marxist claim that the economic is primary. This
claim thereby dissolves into the economic what it sees as the mas-
querade of aesthetic theory. Those claiming such an economic reduction of the aesthetic insist that, within a society that sees all things
possessing value equally as mere commodities, art itself—even "high
art," which basks in the mystique of a special value—is no more than a
commodity.[1] They argue, in effect, that it is not they, the demystifiers

---

[1] I remind you that this treatment of the art work as a commodity that has been
fetishized is an adaptation of Marx's claims about fetishism in the opening chapter
("Commodities") in his *Capital*. (See note 13 to my first lecture.)

of art, who are responsible for reducing the domain of aesthetic value (and aesthetic objects and aesthetic experiences) to the mundane level of material value; it is rather society's own pressure of economic aggrandizement that has reduced qualitative distinctions to quantitative ones, reduced the question of how much better one item is than another to the question of how much more must be paid for it. So it is society, and not its critics, that has corrupted and materialized the concept of value. The function of connoisseurship in the arts has been reduced from the recognition of aesthetic loftiness in objects to investment counseling. If the deprivation of aesthetic value has been accomplished by society itself in its own coarseness, then these commentators are only reminding us of these rude facts and bringing the role assigned to art by our theory into line with the role assigned to art by social-economic forces within an acquisitive society. The art object is a commodity among commodities, a "good" among society's "goods," with the word "good" (or "goods") clearly economic in meaning and function, and no longer suffering the pretense to any distinction in the realm of qualitative value. Under the ruthless candor of their critique, such commentators go on to argue, it will no longer be possible for culture hypocritically to maintain a metacommodity status for objects it has deceptively been holding out as sacred. These new gods—the secular substitutes for the literal gods demythified by earlier critiques—are no more immune than the older ones to positivistic exposure.

From the dissolution of art into economic fact political action should follow. Once brought down, without discrimination, to the world of quantity, all commodities should, on democratic principles, be egalitarianized. Art must be placed on the level with non-art, since there is in theory no reason *not* to do so. There seems, in other words, to be a moral justification for suppressing distinctions in value among our art objects. Without worrying about taking too literally an analogy between a classless society of persons and a classless society of their products, such anti-aesthetic critics blithely hold that class structures should no longer be tolerated among our commodities any more than they are among our citizens. And what betrays this outmoded class consciousness more than the act of setting apart a few select masterworks into a "canon," a term whose unfortunate theological implications can now be exploited? In the domain of commodities there can obviously be no intrinsic qualities to argue for masterworks or for a canon made up of them. We have seen the avant-garde enemies to the aesthetic literalize (and thus reduce to raw economics) the submerged economic metaphors in discussions about aesthetic "value" or "worth." Similarly, they see political (and theological) metaphors—on behalf of "privileged" treatment of "elite" members of the "canon"—as implicit everywhere in older and traditional criticism; and they press such metaphors to their literal consequences, since they wish to condemn the aesthetic convention—out of which older cultural moments produced their masterworks—for its aristocratic exclusiveness. And those works most admired in the past are considered to be as obsolete as the discarded social and political institutions that are reflected in their elitist pretensions to be high art.

Such a reduction of art to just one among all our equal commodities is a universal reduction to a "single principle" strangely reminiscent of the Abbé Charles Batteux's treatise of 1746, which I mentioned in my first lecture. I say "strangely" because the current reduction stems from an egalitarian principle, while the eighteenth-century reduction managed to co-exist with a highly stratified conception of society and function. It is the universalism that the two strategies have in common. I am suggesting only that the new radicalism in criticism, for all its anti-elitism, can in some ways be viewed as a reactionary movement, harking back to critical structures that preceded the distinctions among the arts that came with their liberation in the nineteenth century.

This current reduction of art—or of all symbolic expression—to a single principle constitutes a revulsion against history, a denial of the great works of past periods. In its desire to deconstruct the notion of aesthetic value, the new radicalism in criticism turns against the concept of an elite corps of art works. Such discriminations in value are now treated as if we were dealing with distinctions among citizens within a social structure. To reject our revered masterpieces, then, is really to reject the political institutions at work in the cultures that produced them. It is as if, by turning against an aesthetic monument, which history and the critical tradition have carefully segregated—and lifted above—its fellows, the anti-elitist critics can somehow wish out of existence the reactionary political context that may have been thriving when the work was created. (And they find it hard to ignore the fact that much of our highest art has emerged out of reactionary political moments.) Better yet, these anti-elitists are implicitly acknowledging that, if the work should have any special endowments, those endowments require, and grow out of, the undemocratic characteristics of its social-political context, so that, by denying what had been the accepted superiority of the work, the anti-elitists can somehow discredit the political beliefs of the culture behind it. Hardly a sample of "people's art," the great work of "high art" seems to demand the metaphors of an aristocratic body politic even to find the audacity to ask for itself the privileged treatment, the idolatry, that has been accorded it.

If, then, in this egalitarian society, there are to be no specially valued entities (that is, entities valued for their difference in kind, and not just their differences in degree, from other entities), aesthetic value—as more than material and, hence, as qualitative—becomes a phantom whose existence the skeptical will deny. Accordingly, we find that sympathetic commentators on modern art tend to welcome all comers equally, disdaining the role of qualitative discrimination. They see this role as obsolete and as foreign to their newer obligation to be fully aware—without discrimination—of all objects and actions that reflect contemporary experience. If the world itself is to be our museum, its everyday objects are equally worthy of the critics' attention because they are equally expressive of the lives behind them. The term "discrimination," again, is given a political flavor and, accordingly, is abhorred. An ungenerous observer of these commentators (the word "critics" is really unjustified in view of the uncritical and universally receptive nature of so much of their commentary) might suggest that their antipathy to the notion of aesthetic value and the elite objects of which such value could be predicated springs from a fear of evaluation arising out of the increasing variety of things appearing every day—bizarre and not bizarre—to which they must be receptive or lose their claim to being unqualifiedly avant-garde. (Among academics in the field of art, those dealing with contemporary phenomena seem to be without restraint in insisting on universal receptivity and rejecting the act of judgment, since historian-critics seem mainly to restrict *their* activities to periods whose works are susceptible to iconographic interpretation, which remains their primary interest. So the commentators on the "new" are left as free with today's art as all the activities included within the arts are left free to admit almost anything into their ranks. In return, these commentators refrain from intruding upon the past, the domain of the historian-critic, whose special object, filled with illusionary objects, would not interest the commentators on the "new" in any case.)

One important consequence of denying the status of art to specially formed objects is the denial also of any kind of formal closure in the object as an aesthetic criterion to be searched out by the critic. From Kant onward, this formal finality had been the fulfillment of our aesthetic need to find internal purposiveness in the object. The dethroning of aesthetic object and aesthetic value and the abolition altogether of the aesthetic realm destroy the closed sanctity of such objects as self-fulfilled, instead opening them anew to an immediate relationship to normal experience. With the theoretical disappearance of closure, which is now seen to have been a deceiving myth, all objects, their would-be fictional boundaries dissolved, flow freely into and out of normal experience, now that they are declared no more than a routine part of that experience. John Dewey's book, *Art as Experience,*[2] in effect becomes more of a slogan for what has happened than he could ever have intended (since he retained a strong commitment to the heavy weight of aesthetic dominance of both the art object and our experience of it).

One sees an obvious reflection of these tendencies in the emergence of "action painting" and of "pop art" in the years following the Second World War. As in Dewey, these movements yield a great deal to the desire to merge both the production and experiencing of art with common experience, while they still retain—even at their most iconoclastic—some interest in the artifact that finally emerges. In action painting, centered as it is on the act rather than on the product, there is a devotion to the freedom and spontaneity of the creative process that seeks ways to have that process itself function as the object. This emphasis on spontaneity— on accident rather than on deliberate form—leads to analogues in other arts: on "happenings" instead of dramas, on "environments" instead of sculptures. Nevertheless, in these cases there is in the end a subtle and unintended deference paid to the aesthetic occasion: the continual at-

[2]*Art as Experience* (New York: Minton, Balch & Company, 1934).

tempt to aim at the accidental or the random becomes, in spite of itself, a formal act; and works of art, seeking to dissolve into process, yet present themselves separately from the outside world for our approval of them.

Similarly, the paradox of pop art—in effect collages made up of bits and pieces of the workaday world—is that it wants to have everything both ways, as not art at all and yet as a work of art. Braque and Picasso, we must remember, much earlier had produced purely formalist collages out of everyday materials; but pop art was to offer the materials themselves, supposedly without any formal redisposition of them. It used either the imitation of everyday materials, or (even more extremely) the materials themselves, to urge the obliteration of any line between art and life, to urge—that is—the anti-aesthetic character of our culture's commercialism. Yet at the same time what could be more divorced from the direct satisfaction of any "interest" (yes, even in Kant's sense of the word) than the ripping of these materials from their worldly context in order to display them within the context of an art object? For an art "object" the product does remain (as the statistics of sales and prices of pop art should assure us).

As I suggested, it does not matter whether the objects with which pop art deals are imitations of objects of everyday life or the materials of everyday life themselves (say, pictured cans of soup or actual soup cans). The second, the direct appropriation of things rather than just the literal imitation of things, can be seen as emphasizing only more dramatically the difference between art and life instead of the blending of them: for even the real thing itself, torn from the environment in which it does its worldly job and taken over as part of the art work, becomes but an imitation of itself insofar as it was defined by its usual function, in its proper context, of satisfying a worldly interest. It thus shouts the separateness of the art object of which it is a part even more loudly than would its painted imitation, since, by definition, the painted imitation acknowledges from the start its illusionary—as mimetic—basis. So pop art, the more it relies on real items from the real world, only exaggerates the art's artifice even while it apparently seeks to collapse it into the normal stuff of living. It was, as we shall see, to take a movement beyond pop art to complete the obliteration of the realm of art, its objects, its museums—to have everything immersed within the indivisible flood of experience.

56

Today the museum, an archaic structure authorized by an archaic aesthetic, must itself be insecure, and even apologetic, about the separate nature of its existence and of its relation to contemporary experience. An extraordinary example of this awareness can be seen in the recent, and highly controversial, Centre Georges Pompidou in Paris (informally called Beaubourg, the place where it was built). By calling itself a "centre" rather than a museum, it means to emphasize its function in its culture: it sees itself as an ongoing function rather than as a mere repository, though it has gathered a good number of works for permanent display and would, if it could, gather more of those that have been held out by those whom the Centre offends. Still, it prefers to see itself as a set of social functions instead of as a separate thing, though it stands so grotesquely apart from its environment and must have its architectural character (as a thing) debated, whether it is attacked as a monstrosity or defended as an efficient machine for culture. At once a museum and not a museum, a separate structure holding precious objects and a set of ongoing interactions with its surrounding society, it cannot make up its mind about the thoroughness with which it would break down its walls. Not that there is any question about its commitment to a relationship with its culture radically more intimate than what the older aesthetic envisaged. The inside is to merge with the outside and not begin—maintaining its integral space—only where the latter is locked out.

The rationale for this notion is provided throughout the Centre's own publications, especially in the pamphlet, *A Key to the Georges Pompidou Centre*.[3] Here, for example, is the author's justification of the Centre's piazza, its outside reception area:

> . . . With their Piazza, the architects created, so to speak, a *Pre-Centre*. The Pompidou Centre begins not inside, but outside on this pedestrians square which dips gently down to the doors of the Centre. . . .
>
> Although before and during the Middle Ages, art was associated with religion, it was still community and public orientated. In the course of time, cultural activities on the streets disappeared. Art was enclosed in museums. It became associated with attendants locking doors and with silent rooms, whereas its roots lay with noisy popular festivals.
>
> An open space within the heart of the city, the Piazza recreates this popular dimension but in a secular parvis which can bring to the

[3]Catherine Roux, *A Key to the Georges Pompidou Centre* (Paris: Centre Georges Pompidou, 1978).

Museum a little noise and a little fresh air. The numerous activities which take place in the street and in real life, while extending the notion of culture to the village fete, will tempt the passer-by to stop, linger, familiarize himself with art forms and perhaps come in. (p. 9)

The final four words ("and *perhaps* come in") are to emphasize the insufficiency of the building itself, which is fighting its enclosure, having become a system of functions rather than a repository.[4] The author, in the current fashion, accompanies the rejection of the usual museum concept with an aversion to the fetishizing of art objects, which she sees as a constant threat. She tells us that the term "parvis"—as church courtyard—might have been used as an appropriate designation for the piazza's decentering function, "but that would have again been giving art a sacred connotation"—obviously reason enough to discard the idea at once.

The pamphlet closes with the vision of the Centre's new function and the new art to which it can help give rise: "At Beaubourg, for the first time, the public is able to relate Art to contemporary Life; a simple transparent facade separates the two. Thus, the outside life of Paris joins with the life inside the Centre forming a merger which may perhaps give rise to new art forms" (p. 31). One of the new forms to which it is intended to give rise can be seen in the special combinations of materials brought together for spectacular exhibitions like "Paris-New York" and "Paris-Berlin" in the Centre's early years. In these the objects of art are thoroughly immersed in a profusion of cultural materials addressed to the several senses and to the theoretical and historical imaginations. They constitute a display of mixed media that overruns the halls and floors of the building, mixing the arts together and—more important—mixing arts and humanity's broadly social experience in compartments that melt into one another. The blending of the materials of art and life, and the manipulation of space to allow the blending to occur, suffuse the atmosphere with the motley moment of time and space that is represented.

These exhibitions themselves can be seen as a new art form if we take seriously the kind of art called for by the fairly recent movement

---

[4]It is just this decentering of a repository of elements into a system of functions that post-structuralism calls for in its analysis of language. This is to anticipate my discussion of the second group, those who deal with the verbal arts. Still, it seemed worthwhile to point out the similarity of aesthetic temperament between the motives behind the Beaubourg and those that move recent semiotics.

of "conceptualism." The movement completes the drift of theory away from its identification of art with an object. I have observed the ambivalence in the attitudes toward art in apparently revolutionary movements, which try to break down barriers between experience and events on the one hand and art on the other, but which still retain some devotion to an object. But the retreat from aesthetic form proceeded beyond "abstract expressionism" (a movement which, from current perspectives, seems rather traditionally devoted to a sense of the object) and later movements like action painting and pop art; the retreat seemed to find its extreme form in "minimalism," but the utter extremity of conceptualism may well be either its final statement or its final parody. In conceptualism almost anything is permitted *except* an art object: primarily conceptualists seek art in the ideas that lead to actions, events, or organizations of things or even factual data. It has managed what, in the title of Lucy Lippard's booklength report and anthology, she terms, in the spirit of conceptualism, "the dematerialization of the art object."[5]

This disappearance of the object has taken us as far from the traditional aesthetic as we can go. It represents what I think of as a new declaration of the non-objective character of art, a declaration far more radical than the earlier call for non-objective art (by which, however radical such calls then sounded to us, was meant only non-representational art, art without represented objects in it). The confusion between the two kinds of non-objectivity is the negative side of what has been a long-standing ambiguity in discussions about art and objects since the earliest days of art theory in the West. For many centuries literary critics, working parasitically from criticism of the visual arts, were controlled by the theory of imitation, which required them to talk about the work of art as an assemblage of imitated objects rather than as an integral object itself. A major result of Kant's aesthetic of internal purposiveness was that it shifted the meaning of "object" to the art work from the external items collected, in imitative form, within it. Both these meanings of "object" are with us yet to haunt our description of what has been happening in what we used to call the plastic arts. Earlier in this century the revolution against representational objects could have been viewed only as a desire to

[5]*Six Years: The Dematerialization of the Art Object from 1966 to 1972,* ed. Lucy R. Lippard (New York: Frederick A. Praeger, 1973). See also Ursula Meyer, *Conceptual Art* (New York: E. P. Dutton, 1972).

force iconographically oriented art commentators to recognize that the "object" was to be nothing less than the art work itself as a construct, and not as an imitated item within the work. Thus non-objective art in this sense hardly threatened the aesthetic in its formal-istic focus on elite objects separated from the common world; on the contrary, it meant to solidify this claim. (The work might forfeit the double vision of objects that, as I pointed out toward the end of my first lecture, representational works can claim, even as literature can: the objects as existing prior to the work and the objects as reconsti-tuted to function within a work that has constituted itself as its own object. So the representational work uses both meanings of "object," at once containing objects and being an object itself. The non-objective work in the original sense forgoes the first but retains the second the more forcefully, asserting its formal being as a construct while disdaining iconographic interest as being no more than pre-aesthetic.)

But the artistic (or rather anti-artistic) activity that follows from the recent tendencies that lead to conceptualism claims to be non-objective in the truly radical sense: it insists that art work, as an idea or as an activity stemming from an idea, does not produce objects at all. Such an insistence, to the extent that it is held with theoretical purity (in spite of all common-sense resistance), represents the final undoing of the entire post-Kantian aesthetic. And, incidentally, to the extent that such ideas were to be successfully imposed, the art marketplace would be eliminated along with the precious objects it capitalized upon by mythologizing them and creating an aesthetic to justify them. All come tumbling down together.

I now turn to the second of the two groups (which I mentioned at the start) who seek to demystify criticism's idolatry of the arts. These are the recent theorists of the verbal arts who are concerned not with the corruption and consequent deception represented by valuable mate-rial objects but with the poetic word that earlier critics came to treat as sacred. We saw in my first lecture that recent criticism of the language arts shares the leveling impulse found in criticism of the plastic arts, even though words do not share the misleading worldly value of material objects. I suggested there that one could argue either way, that the immaterial nature of poetry could—through inversions pro-duced by Freudian subtlety—be shown to be a displacement that only strengthened the traditional aesthetic's devotion to the splendor of the art object as a sacred body, or that the immaterial nature of poetry furnished obvious evidence against the Marxist attempt to discredit the aesthetic by reducing it to crassly economic motives. In any case, the "word" itself, spoken and written, has a sufficiently lengthy association with magic, with sacred texts, and with fleshly incarnations, for demythologizing critics to find plenty of stimulus for applying reductive instruments without resorting to the economic argument based on material artifacts ("commodities"). As I have anticipated (and warned) in my previous lectures, the impetus driving literary critics to purge the poem of its elite attributions derives largely from the fact that the poem and their own work both use words; and this leads critics to the mistaken notion that both have the same medium. The poem, then, can be deprived of any sanctity as an object once critics remind us of the general ways in which language functions. For they no longer allow for any exemption for poetry from these ways, having armed themselves against claims made by the traditional aesthetic in the name of poetry's "deviationist" nature, which provided it with *its* language as a special medium.[6]

What immediately seems to militate against the poem's functioning as an object is the openness of language: each text opens toward the world that it presumably signifies, each text opens to other texts whose verbal elements it redisposes, and each text opens to the author who uses it to satisfy personal needs by creating it and to the reader who must interpret its signs into personal meanings if these signs are to function. Every one of these open functions is performed wherever language operates, so that every one of them can furnish a different argument for deconstructing any text that claims a privilege based on closure.

As we have seen in my second lecture, self-inflating critics, having leveled the poem's language with their own, can make themselves rivals to the poet, seeking to assert their own egos and their own

---

[6]In my first lecture, I tried to show how the notion that language in poetry deviates from normal usage is central to the theorist's argument that allows poetry to conform to the traditional aesthetic by finding for it a medium analogous to the media of the plastic arts. I treat this issue at length and with some self-criticism in my essay, "Literature vs. *Ecriture*: Constructions and Deconstructions in Recent Critical Theory," *Studies in the Literary Imagination*, 12 (1979), pp. 1–17. See especially pp. 8–11.

meanings, at whatever cost to the poem. In the manner of Harold Bloom, these critics would unmask the culture's idolatry for the works of our fathers by openly confronting the Freudian nature of the family narrative that others call literary history. The inevitable ego-sponsored act of misreading (a necessary and therefore justified act of misreading) is the critic's obvious way to dissolve the object into the radical temporality of the reader's experience of it.

The license given to readers in more extreme versions of reader-reception theory these days suggests that there is almost no stability permitted to reside in the words of a poem and therefore almost no control given to the poem's context over the reader's response. This is pretty much to turn on its head the New-Critical claim that the task of the poem was ever to tighten its context, moving toward total closure in order to impose that context upon the reader's, thereby narrowing the range of the reader's responses. The New-Critical argument was simply that maximal control by an objective context would produce minimal variations of response. Inversely, those who now would permit maximal freedom in the reader's response must claim minimal stability and control in the text. Their argument, deriving from the general way language works, ends by turning all poems into forms of "minimal art," a notion obviously similar to the movement in the visual arts to which I earlier referred as "minimalism." And, as in the case of the visual arts, the emancipation of the reader or audience—the equal authority of their discourse and the creative artist's—is purchased only by the diminishing of the object toward its "zero degree."

There is a far larger and more persuasive body of critics these days who would deprive the poem of its peculiarly aesthetic nature by dwelling upon its openness to all other discourse and to the language system at large, in effect deconstructing all texts into undifferentiated textuality. What I am referring to is the wave of "structuralist" and "post-structuralist" thinking, largely imported from France, as it has affected attitudes about literature or rather, in many instances, attitudes *against* literature as a definable entity. In its most influential form these days, structuralism treats *écriture* (writing) as a single, blanket term, and has tended to collapse all distinctions others might make within *écriture* as it seeks the single syntactical principle that, homologously from discourse to discourse, accounts for the disposition of elements within each. All instances of discourse, of whatever sort and in whatever field, are treated equally as subjects for structuralist analysis. To put this reduction another way, all are seen as instances of *paroles,* equally answerable to the *langue* that licenses them. If our penchant for mystification leads us to honor some of these with the name of poems and to treat them as sacred objects with self-enclosed systems, structuralists would demystify the fetish as they deconstruct the aesthetic that authorizes it. Even an attempt to distinguish among the affective varieties of speech acts (as other recent theorists suggest) usually finds the poetic leveled into the manipulative capacities of language at large.

If all of language, conceived as a system of signs, is seen as one universal structure, then any writing sample—regardless of subject or intention or method—must be similarly treated for interpretive purposes as part of that single code, with predictable relationships both among its signs and between its signs and the meanings to which they pretend. It would follow that no writing sample has privilege over any other, that none can finally claim to be a sovereign entity cut off from the rest as a system unto itself. Further, the code that determines the workings of written signs may be applied to other symbolic human relations as well, so that all sorts of social situations—in life as in word—may be treated as texts. Everything is a text, even as—really—nothing is a text, since it would be more accurate to say that everything is an intertext. In the midst of such a ubiquity of texts within a single, seamless fabric of textuality, we should indeed be hard put to mark off an area that we could call "literature" or, for that matter, even to claim any isolable verbal artifacts as special objects of study.

What this enterprise has been seeking to accomplish is a deconstruction of the metaphysical assumptions behind the traditional aesthetic and the resulting claim about the poem's ontology: the claim that the poem is a totalized structure, a self-realized teleological closure, a microcosm whose mutually dependent elements are cooperatively present in the fulfillment of their centripetal potentialities. Instead, the deconstructive move reduces the poem to a play of centrifugal forces. Gaps appear everywhere, and we are to acknowledge these gaps for what they are, resisting our constructive habit—imposed on us by centuries of self-deceiving metaphysical assumptions—of trying at all costs to fill them. For what we have taken to be the work is, like all discourse, mere vacancy, acknowledging an absence of substance, fleeing all presence as it leads us down the lines moving outward to the intertextual forces that become the code, but permit no integrity, no free-standing sovereignty, to any would-be body operating within them. In this sense, the poem, as a construction of elements manipulated by art into a presence (according to the traditional aesthetic), has been deconstructed into absences that can be made to point only to the code of writing itself. But, beyond this statement, we must add that— since the structuralist impulse is always in motion and since, in other words, structuralism should be seen as an activity rather than a position—a further post-structuralist deconstruction must undo the structure of the code as well, lest that become a presence demanding its own metaphysical sanction. And so the deconstructions progress (or, rather, so they continue, since to say they "progress" is to suggest a teleological structure that smuggles in its own metaphysical ground). The deconstructions continue, as we are left increasingly with decentered forces freely at play as discourse moves itself—here again— toward its "zero degree."

However different we have found the philosophical grounds and the purposes of the deconstructive enterprise among theorists in the verbal arts—precisely because it is words and not things that they are dealing with—we observe parallels or similarities between the dematerialization of the object urged by them and that which we saw urged by the theorists in the material and spatial arts. (I have already pointed out echoes between "minimalism" in art and some "reception theory" in literature, and between the decentering impulse in the Pompidou and in post-structuralism.) In none of the tendencies I have described in recent theory of the verbal arts is the object more impressively negated than in the semiotic attempt to move beyond words and to convert all social experience into textual terms. I have mentioned this expansion of strictly verbal signs to a universal behavioral textuality, with all our disciplines, activities, and interrelationships now treated as sign structures calling for interpretation. Thus hermeneutics becomes an omnibus exercise as our journals broaden out from *Semiotexte* to the recently introduced *Social Text*. Having emptied literature into *écriture*, some theorists, still not content, in turn empty *écriture* into the world (verbal and otherwise) as text. It is the verbal critic's equivalent to the museum without walls as the world itself. I cannot think of a closer analogue to what we have observed of "conceptualism" in art than those who would apply textual terms to all social relations. In both cases the submerging of the object, and of verbal or visual signs themselves, into an undifferentiated welter of experience makes the leveling act complete. And yet, as an act, it is never complete: it is an unending act of semiosis that is continually opening outward.

But what of the need for closure felt by the human imagination—the very need on which Kant, in effect, grounded his entire enterprise? In my first lecture, I sought to show ways in which poems could be treated (by the traditional aesthetic) as manipulations and even distortions of language that enable it to create itself as a medium that can close off what structuralists and others have shown to be normally open. The persistent impulse on the part of poets to close the form they create and on our part to close the form we perceive accounts for the purposiveness that, for Kant, characterizes the aesthetic mode.[7]

Presumably it is this need to make or to find closure that leads us to the mythmaking and, with it, the privileging of objects that the anti-elitists—our principal subject in these lectures—have been undermining. For central to their assault on the aesthetic object is their antagonism to the valorizing of humanly created order, the order of the art work, that is traditionally to elevate it above the raw experience it transforms. They see something snobbishly anti-democratic in the aesthete's claim that art creates an order that ordinary life lacks, that art therefore represents a higher realm of human perception to which life without art can never pretend. For here is another attempt to keep art on the heights from which they would lower it.

Instead of the human creator seeking to triumph over ordinary life through the imposition of a created order, anti-elitists—as we have been observing them in these lectures—ask for the embrace of the

[7]This aesthetic of elite objects and closed forms reaches a high point in the brilliance of the giants of "modernism"—among many others, Yeats, Eliot, and Stevens in poetry; Joyce, Proust, and Mann in the novel. They are the major candidates for late entries in the canon. What is often called the "postmodern" may be seen as marking a break and demanding a different aesthetic, or anti-aesthetic, imbued by the iconoclasm that is my subject in these lectures. But it may also turn out that even works composed in rebellion to the post-Kantian aesthetic will be found, in spite of themselves, to have been responsive to formal habits of creation that transcend the conscious intentions prescribed by particular historical periods.

ordinary and condemn any order that would disdain it. As anti-elitists, they distrust as politically suspect our every impulse to refine the ordinary into a transcendent order that would improve aesthetically upon it. Perhaps they have taken all too literally reactionary political arguments in defense of elitism like those of T.S. Eliot in his *Notes Towards the Definition of Culture* (1948). And they respond, appropriately, with antagonism. In relating art to society, anti-elitists also relate aesthetic order to social-political order, believing that a high degree of the first usually has been found where there is a high degree of the second. They are aware that a highly ordered society has hardly been the most progressive; indeed, the unprogressive nature of societies in which our greatest art has been produced is hardly an encouragement to their hopes. Consequently, anti-elitists may well fear that, to the extent that art reflects its culture, the art most conducive to order (our high art) is reflective of a most regressive social order, since it emerged out of such an order. Conversely, the progress of society, with its breakdown of accepted orders in the name of freedom and equality, may well carry with it the subversion of the potential greatness of elite objects of art. And the continuing insistence on producing such objects poses—for such observers—a threat to the progress of the culture art is to reflect, because, if art does indeed reflect its culture, it would still have to work toward a society, however reactionary, within which its own penchant for order felt comfortable.

If, then, society dedicates itself to preserve cultural conditions under which such elite objects can still be produced, must it not put a priority on a social order that may well play against the egalitarian impulse usually associated with social progress? So we can seek to restrict progress in the arts to progress in their capacity to serve—at whatever cost to themselves—progress in a society moving forward toward liberation. Otherwise we seem committed to accept retrograde notions of social order so that we can encourage a still revered aristocratic art. To insist on such an either/or represents a strangely unfortunate surrender of art to society, a surrender based on a simplistic and fearful equation made between aesthetic and social orders, as if "order" was necessarily the same thing in both realms. So, inimical to order as necessarily hierarchical and idolatrous, and in love with indiscriminate, pedestrian experience at large, anti-elitists reject elite art along with the obsolete society and social beliefs that cherish their elites. Anti-elitists have come to accept a newer and literally revolutionary notion of (what, for lack of another term, I shall still call) art, and they see it as more progressive (and hence, in their special sense, better) than the rejected notion of art. They can even claim to find progress in art through the ages leading up to our own lucky moment, although they are speaking of art's function, the immediacy of its relations with a society's total experience, rather than of its rarefied value as a thing in itself, which they have gladly given up.

The commitment to order—and to the humanly created forms that establish it—remains the central commitment of the Kantian tradition, which, as we have seen, must uphold the object and that rarefied value. That tradition holds that the aesthetic order is of its own kind and not necessarily a reflection of any social order. Indeed, its interest in the transformational power of the aesthetic order suggests that this order reshapes, and perhaps even subverts, the general ideas to which social beliefs and structures conform. Of course, it is just this tribute to the autonomy of the art work's aesthetic form that provoked the demystifiers' impatience. Indeed, I have frequently commented here on their charge that such tribute is utter idolatry that turns the work into a fetish whose falsely sacred nature the demystifying critics have exposed. Any attempt by me to return to a traditional defense of the object should confront this charge: it should recognize the extent to which the art work has attributes that call forth a religious-like response, but it should move beyond to recognize also the extent to which it immunizes itself from our confounding it with the sacred.

Since the later nineteenth century, criticism has been advancing the notion of the arts as humanity's substitute for religion: the artist was seen as our substitute for God, with every aesthetic creation, the work of art, the substitute for God's sacred world, the "Book of Nature," each one a secular equivalent of the "Book of Books."[8] The Western mind lost its metaphysical security with the advent of eighteenth-century critical philosophy, which undermined what had seemed to be the safe, ontological assumptions of rationalism. With

---

[8]For a fuller discussion of the relation of the poem (as fully functioning and fully interpretable) to the "Book of Nature," as well as to the even more sacred "Book of Books," see my *Theory of Criticism: A Tradition and Its System* (Baltimore: Johns Hopkins University Press, 1976), pp. 145–48.

the external ground for order and unity removed, future teleological structures would have to emanate from the human imagination. Thus Kant could make the formal purposiveness of the aesthetic object its indispensable characteristic as that object offered itself, with its internal structure—a microcosm calculated to satisfy the human desire for form—as substitute for the macrocosmic security now denied to humanity's cognitive power.

This surrogate aesthetic power of the work clearly depended on its fictional distance from our world, a distance that could ensure its self-sufficiency. Free from the world and bound only to itself, it could satisfy the aesthetic hunger growing out of the human desire for form—once satisfied by a theology and a metaphysic—without having to confront those metaphysical claims that human cognition dared no longer set forth. This anthropological justification of art's role as a surrogate religion, offering its fictional objects for satisfactions that the larger unfictional world can no longer guarantee, is a view that, as I have said, criticism has come to live with for better than a century now. Writers like Matthew Arnold in England and Nietzsche on the Continent were especially influential in establishing this view, which has been extended in many detailed ways in the course of our own century. This development has only enhanced the treatment of art objects as the secular analogues to the now obsolete structures of what had been sacred objects. And the museums containing such objects had indeed, as I have suggested in my first lecture, something of a secular church about them.

The worship of objects within the museum or within our poetic anthologies, as Arnold was the first to remind us, has the characteristic of religious worship in that it satisfies those teleological demands of the mind that religion used to satisfy before disbelief intervened; but, being fictional, the object need not disappoint us as theology did. What is sacred is our approach and response to the soliciting structure of the object, not its substance, to which we are to respond with disinterest. The secular art object is the more valuable—indeed newly indispensable—to the human imagination for going it alone, without a back-up metaphysical claim behind it. This is an indispensability that the religious object of art—in happier days for metaphysics—never had or needed. The secular art object, then, may indeed seem like a fetish as it serves this aesthetic, except that its secular character as a self-conscious fiction is meant to protect it from the excesses of actual fetishism. Still, the successful work of art satisfies our teleological imagination, which will not sleep even when our religious instinct does. What is teleology except the projection of our need to find purpose in the cosmos, macrocosmos or microcosmos: macrocosmos in our theology or in our rationalism or, in retreat from those, microcosmos in the internal completeness of the single art object? This retreat is traced in our aesthetic activities since Kant, who was himself too self-conscious a demythologizer not to warn us against projecting cognitive power onto our aesthetic satisfactions. Art shows us how to see our world, not how to know it; it provides categories of vision, not of knowledge.

Anthropologists tell us nothing that suggests that our human hunger for form looks for its satisfactions any less now—or will need them less in the future—than it has in the past. As the chaos that surrounds us becomes the more threatening, the likelihood is that we will need such formal satisfactions all the more. Indeed even in our more avant-garde moments, as we try to contemplate with pleasure some of the more experimental ventures in art (or anti-art) around us, would we not confess that we do so only while reserving to ourselves the right to seek in older masterworks the formal (even if idolatrous) satisfactions that the aesthetic tradition prescribes? Do we not indulge the latest theatrical "happening" that we witness, secure in our conviction that Shakespeare is still there for us when we call upon him? We may sanction these newer anti-elitist alternatives in the arts, in their flight from form and even from objects themselves, as an egalitarian translation of everything into art (or of art into everything); and we may countenance them as some sort of reflection of our culture's chaotic freedom. But I suggest we do so the more easily because we have the assurance of another sort of art that is still there for us, though that art is now torn away from the cultural values that would sustain it and is, in some subterranean way, serving our culture which, with another violently revolutionary art of its own, probably needs such works more than ever to fall back on. For these lectures I should change this metaphor and move it above ground, and suggest, rather, that the masterworks remain as giants on our leveled landscape, disrupting our flatland with their lofty grace.

The mind's desire to find closure may largely account for the role of the story—like that of the picture frame or the proscenium arch—in the history of culture. The inherent nature of narrative structure surely reveals a responsiveness to what Frank Kermode called our "sense of an ending." The satisfying ending is one that fulfills internally aroused expectations, that realizes the purposes immanent in the story. From Aristotle's concept of denouement or falling action to the formal finality of Kant, and in the formalistic theory that is indebted to both, we find the imposition of a mythic ending, a structural apocalypse that cuts off the fiction from history. It acts, in effect, as an intrusion of the spatial imagination on the radical temporality of pure sequence, shaping time into the separateness of fiction. Linear sequence is thus transformed into circularity. (This roundedness as a habit of narrative structure, is, I fear, reflected in my own story here, as I now have returned to Kant and Kantian purposiveness, seeking to end my story where I began it in my first lecture, thereby effecting some degree of closure.)

But there is something in literature that also keeps it open to the world, to language at large, and to the reader. I have earlier dealt at length with the two-sided nature of words once they have been shaped into a poetic medium: they try to work their way into a self-sufficient presence, and yet they remain transient and empty signifiers. I noted that the differences between language and the plastic media—the prior meanings of language and its lack of materiality—at first may seem to put language at a disadvantage as a medium, but I noted also that its duplicity opens special capacities in it that may permit it to become a model medium for the others. It can do so by exploiting its paradoxical nature. That is, language is able, like other media, to create itself into a fiction, but, because it is also only no more than language—just words after all—it is able to display a self-consciousness about its illusionary character. It seems to be both full of itself and empty, both totally here as itself and pointing elsewhere, away from itself. It permits its reader at once to cherish its creation as a closed object, one that comes to terms with itself, and to recognize its necessarily incomplete nature in its dependence on us as its readers, on literary history, on the general language system, and on the way of the world. We can see its words as uniquely apart from the world and the world of language, while we see them also as blending into those worlds.

In other words, the literary work persuades us of itself as a special object even as we retain an awareness of the rather extraordinary activity we are performing in contributing to our own persuasion. It is not fetishism when we recognize the tentative conditions that encourage the closure we celebrate, and when we accept the openness that surrounds the moment of our commitment to the closed object. Language, considered in this light, can lead us to accompany our aesthetic indulgence with skepticism, to tie art to life while we give it its special due. It is thus that I propose language, converted into literature's medium, as a model medium for the other arts. If criticism can see the other arts as also exploiting their media through a self-conscious duplicity (and Gombrich has helped show us ways in which artists enhance their awareness of illusion), then these arts can also be treated as more—and as less—than a fetish. The other arts may well follow the lead of literature in moving beyond commodity status, moving from artifact to art.

I feel, obviously, that many of the demythologizing tendencies in our recent theory may be healthy, provided they do not end by taking discriminations in value—or, worse, the objects themselves—from us. It is good for theory to be more conscious than it used to be of the idols it uncritically assumed. So I would hardly suggest that we try to return to the unquestioning confidence we once had in the critical enterprise before we had to respond to the awarenesses aroused by recent antagonistic theory. The recognition by critics of their own fictions, together with the limits of the aesthetic fictions they at once create and uncover for us, gives them a self-deconstructive shrewdness that can only increase our confidence in their more grandiose claims. But, in the end, however persistent their reservations, it is the critics' power to lift that art object off the level and to reconstruct it at its full height that sustains us as it sustains their culture and the uneven arts themselves.

The Hodges Lectures

THE BETTER ENGLISH FUND was established in 1947 by John C. Hodges, Professor of English, The University of Tennessee, 1921–1962, and head of the English Department, 1941–1962, on the returns from the *Harbrace College Handbook,* of which he was the author. Over the years, it has been used to support the improvement of teaching and research in the English Department. The Hodges Lectures are intended to commemorate this wise and generous bequest.

Volumes Published
Theodore Roosevelt Among the Humorists: W. D. Howells, Mark Twain, and Mr. Dooley, by William M. Gibson (1980)

THE HODGES LECTURES book series is set in ten-point Sabon type with two-point spacing between the lines. Sabon is also used for display. The series format was designed by Jim Billingsley. This title in the series was composed by Williams of Chattanooga, Tennessee, printed by Thomson-Shore, Inc., Dexter, Michigan, and bound by John H. Dekker & Sons, Grand Rapids, Michigan. The paper on which the book is printed bears the watermark of S.D. Warren and is designed for an effective life of at least 300 years.

THE UNIVERSITY OF TENNESSEE PRESS : KNOXVILLE